The Aborigines

THE ABORIGINES

Fourth Edition

R.M. Gibbs

LONGMAN

Addison Wesley Longman Australia Pty Limited
95 Coventry Street
South Melbourne 3205 Australia

Offices in Sydney, Brisbane,
Perth, and associated companies
throughout the world.

Cover designed by Mary Kerr
Set in 11/13 Palatino
Produced by Addison Wesley Longman Australia Pty Limited
Printed in Malaysia through Longman Malaysia, LWP

National Library of Australia
Cataloguing-in-Publication data

Gibbs, R.M. (Ronald Malcolm), 1938–
    The Aborigines.

    4th ed.
    Bibliography.
    Includes index.
    ISBN 0 582 80836 7

994.0049915

Cover photo: *"Rainbow Dreaming" by Barney Daniels Tjungurrayi:*
Gallery Gondwana, Alice Springs

Preface

This book provides an introductory survey of the origin and culture of the Aboriginal people of Australia. It also surveys the impact of the white invasion of the continent on traditional Aboriginal society. Its purpose is to encourage a student or general reader to focus on broad questions: above all, what kind of society did Aborigines create in Australia, and what has happened to it? The reading list gives a selection of books to help those who need more specific information. Readers of this book should take into account that in a general book of this kind few examples can be given of local cultural variations and reactions to white settlement.

Care has been taken, out of respect for Aboriginal sacred life, to exclude any material, including illustrations, which may be of a sacred kind and the knowledge of which should be restricted. In some Aboriginal communities advice should be sought about whether further restriction should be placed on some material. It should also be noted that, although the term 'Aborigines' itself is considered inappropriate in some communities and local terms are used instead, the term has been retained in this book to avoid confusion for students.

A book of this kind owes an obvious debt to the work of others, especially in sections dealing with traditional Aboriginal society. Acknowledgement is especially made of the help of Robert Edwards, formerly Curator of Anthropology at the South Australian Museum, and of the assistance of Aboriginal Curriculum Unit staff in the Education Department of South Australia.

Acknowledgments

Acknowledgment is due to the following for permission to reproduce copyright material: Aboriginal Welfare Board Collection, NSW State Archives, courtesy AIATSIS, for the photograph on p. 111; *The Advertiser*, Adelaide, for the photographs on pp. 117, 120, 131; *The Age*, for the photographs on pp. 125, 132; reproduced by permission of the Australian National Gallery, Canberra, for the photograph on p. 72; Australian Picture Library/S. Thomann for the photograph on p. 129; Collection: Tasmanian Museum and Art Gallery, for the line drawing on p. 17 (bottom); D.J. Mulvaney, Australian National University, for the photograph on p. 9; Jacaranda Wiley for permission to reproduce 'A Song of Hope', by Oodgeroo of the tribe Noonuccal (formerly known as Kath Walker) in *My People*, 3rd Edition, 1990, published by Jacaranda Press, p. 138; La Trobe Collection, State Library of Victoria, for photographs on pp. 5, 94 (top), 99, 100; Macmillan, London, for the photographs on pp. 56, 73; The Mortlock Library, State Library of South Australia for the photographs on pp. 23, 39, 60, 70, 103, 106, 107, 109 (permission for photograph on p. 109 also given by Gloria Jean Peterson); *The News*, Adelaide, for the photographs on pp. 117, 120, 131; *News Ltd*, for the photograph on p. 137; Ray Kennedy/*The Age*, for the photograph on p. 136; Ray Titus, *The News*, Adelaide, for the photograph on p. 134; Robert Edwards, for the photographs on pp. 4, 6, 7, 18, 26, 28 (top), 37, 41, 42, 46, 49, 50, 51, 57, 67, 78, 79, 80, 81, 82.

While every effort has been made to trace and acknowledge copyright, in some cases copyright proved untraceable. Should any infringement have occurred, the publishers tender their apologies and invite copyright owners to contact them.

Contents

ABORIGINES: THE FIRST SETTLERS

1

'The settlement of Australia began in 1788.' To many Australians this is a familiar statement, part of the story of their country's foundation and development. It has been white Australians who have put forward this idea. In doing so they have suggested that Australia's history really begins when white people settled the continent. White Australians strengthened this impression in 1988 by holding bicentennial celebrations throughout the nation. But the truth of the matter is different, for human settlement in Australia began with other people. The first Australians had dark skins, not white. They were the ancestors of present-day Aboriginal Australians.

For tens of centuries Aborigines were virtually the only human occupiers of the Australian continent. A few Indonesian traders were seasonal visitors on the north-west coast, and there were some contacts with people from New Guinea and possibly further away. Yet there was almost certainly no attempt by other peoples to settle permanently in Australia before Europeans began to do so late in the eighteenth century. As sole possessors of Australia the Aborigines had developed a highly organised pattern of living. It was not a static pattern but subject to change. They also developed, in their 'Dreaming', their own stories of Australia's history and passed them on to their children. In those stories they explained the origins of their country and their own presence within it.

The Puzzle About Origins

What are the origins of the country and of Aboriginal life within it? Did the Aboriginal people originate in

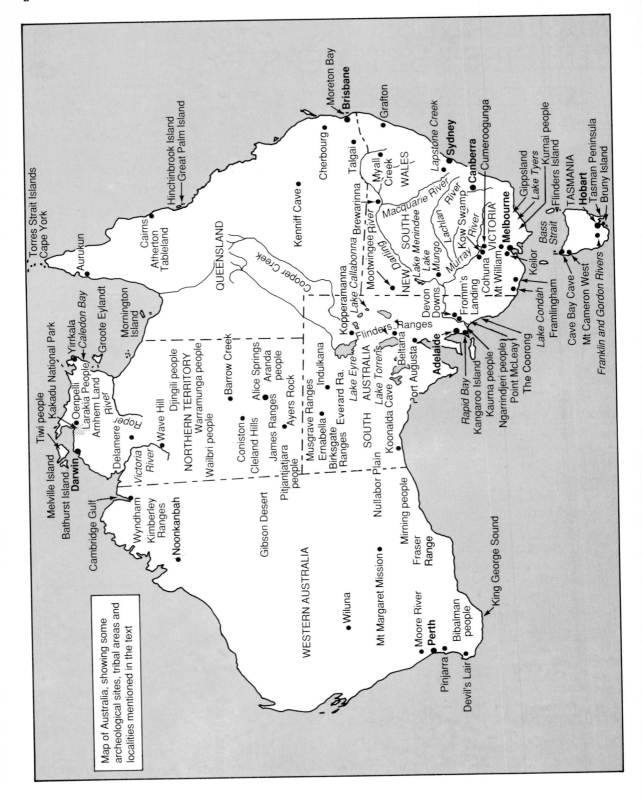

Map of Australia, showing some archeological sites, tribal areas and localities mentioned in the text

Australia? If not, where did they come from? How and why did they come? Did they come together as a single group, or in several groups over a period of time? How many came? What was Australia like when they arrived? These are merely a few of the puzzling questions about origins.

The Dreaming

Aborigines living in their traditional societies have found answers to these questions in their stories of the Dreaming, explaining the relationship between humans and the land. The Dreaming deals with space and also time, and takes in both the past and the present. It includes the period at the dawn of time when the earth was not formed as now but was more like a great plain stretching to the horizon. This was the creation period, when great spirit-ancestors rose from the plain where they had been sleeping. Taking the form of animals such as the kangaroo, snake or eaglehawk, they wandered the earth, behaving almost as humans, until this part of the Dreaming suddenly ended. Some spirit-ancestors went into the sky and others into waterholes or the earth, leaving behind signs of their earthly existence. These were in the form of caves, hills, rivers, holes in rocks, and other natural features of the landscape.

Yet the spirit-ancestors did more than this. They left behind the spirits that were to bring about life in human, plant or animal form, as well as laws, fire, and the first weapons and implements to help Aborigines live on the earth. Aborigines and living things have thus been descendants of these ancestral beings ('Dreaming Beings') and can be said to have personal 'Dreamings'. The ancestral beings themselves did not really die, but lived on in different forms. Nor in Aboriginal belief did the spirits of later Aborigines die—death is merely a physical end, so that a person's spirit survives. The past is thus linked vitally to the present and is very real.

In traditional Aboriginal societies—and among urban Aborigines today—people have believed strongly in the idea of the Dreaming and its general pattern of creation. This idea has explained the past and formed a vital part of their religion, making clear the origins of living things, human and non-human. These origins are recounted in the great stories about the creation period and its spirit-

The Lightning Brothers, painted on a cave wall, Delamere Station, Northern Territory. Yagtchadbulla, on the left, is about 3.5 metres high; with his brother Tcaibuinji he was associated with rain

ancestors. These stories, varying across the continent, have passed down through generations of Aboriginal people, who in turn made them the subjects of important rituals.

Some stories have told of the deeds of an honoured spirit-ancestor, known by names such as *Biami* in parts of New South Wales, as *Bunjil* (the eaglehawk) in central and western Victoria, and as *Biamban*, *Goin* and *Nurelli* elsewhere. Along the lower River Murray there is the belief in *Ngurunderi*, who made the river itself and features of the Murray Valley. In northern areas of the continent, rivers and gorges marked the path of the Rainbow Serpent across the land. Aborigines painted the image of the Rainbow Serpent (known as *Ngalyod* or by other names) in Arnhem Land caves; in caves in the Kimberley Ranges there remain figures of the huge *Wandjina* spirit-ancestors, the makers of lightning, thunder and rain. Another honoured ancestral being has been the Earth Mother, who it was believed came from islands north of Australia. Her spirit-children were the ancestors of different Aboriginal groups. Important rituals, such as the *Kunapipi* ceremonies in northern Australia, developed about this idea. In these ceremonies, held in the dry season, ideas of rebirth and fertility were stressed. These rituals, reverently performed, spread widely.

A tree-carving of Biami

Tracing the Past

Non-Aboriginal Australians—of a different, and usually European, cultural background—have suggested other explanations about the land and its first inhabitants. But explanations are difficult. Time has hidden much evidence concerning early Australia. If Aborigines once migrated to Australia, the seas must now cover a good part of the land they could have traversed. No written records survive about such migration. In recent times Aborigines do not seem to have lived in lands near Australia. Thus it is hard for people of a different cultural background to confirm Aboriginal stories which tell of early migrations of spirit-ancestors into Australia by canoe from the north and indicate that the Aboriginal people originated beyond Australia. It is also hard to confirm other stories which say that the Aboriginal people actually originated in the continent itself.

Many material items, however, have been found at archaeological and other sites. These items suggest what

Disintegrating engravings of human figures on a rockface, Mootwingee, western New South Wales

Aboriginal life was like before Europeans arrived and lead to ideas about the origins of the Aboriginal people. Weapons and implements have frequently been found. Remains such as stone tools, cooking hearths, anvil stones, shells and animal bones have been discovered at former campsites. Tree scars reveal the source for bark objects as large as a canoe. Sacred items have survived, indicating the nature of religious life and its importance. Examples of old art remain, such as engravings and paintings on a variety of surfaces, though some are growing faint due to weathering and vandalism. Koonalda Cave on the Nullarbor Plain has wall markings over 20 000 years old and rather similar to prehistoric markings in European caves, while a recent find of ochre 'crayon' in Arnhem Land has been dated back as far as 60 000 years—perhaps the oldest evidence of art in the world.

These discoveries have been the fruit of archaeological research. This important work requires not only searching and frequent excavating but determining the age of items found. Without knowing the age of items, those who follow European ways of interpreting the past can make little sense of the order of events, leaving the past, with its puzzles about Aboriginal origins and early Australia, a mystery.

Archaeological Research and Dating Techniques

Archaeological research has illuminated the past elsewhere in the world. In the nineteenth century Heinrich

A canoe tree, Blanchetown, South Australia

Schliemann in Turkey revealed the ruins of the fabled city of Troy and other cities. In Australia archaeologists have not had the excitement of finding lost cities. But they have unlocked clues to ancient Australia, in many places finding traces of Aboriginal life in layers of debris materials, just as the archaeologists digging at Troy and other famous sites found layer upon layer of the remains of older civilisations. A pioneering effort in Australia came in 1929, when N.B. Tindale and H.M. Hale excavated a site in a cliff rock shelter at Devon Downs along the lower River Murray. They found twelve layers of remains, revealing at least three different cultural stages of Aboriginal life and suggesting that separate migrations of Aborigines occurred in early times.

Since that time, and especially in recent decades, Australian archaeologists have made further discoveries, several in caves. At Kenniff Cave in southern Queensland flake tools and stencil markings are signs of Aboriginal occupation there, dating from 19 000 years ago. The same cave has yielded smaller stone tools from a much later period. In Koonalda Cave in western South Australia, where the Aboriginal finger-line markings appear in the white walls, Aborigines descended possibly to look for

Ancient finger markings in the walls of Koonalda Cave, western South Australia

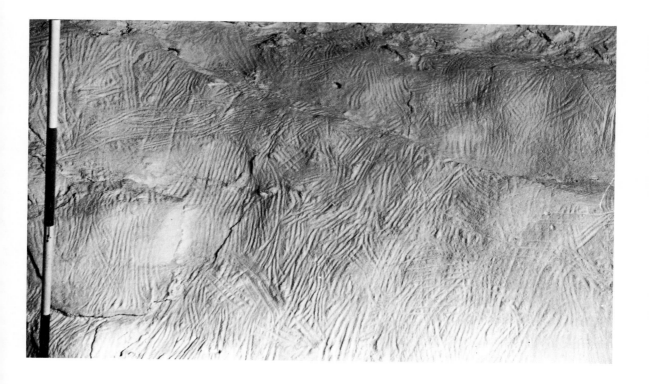

water and seek hard flint for weapons and cutting tools. In Cave Bay Cave on Hunter Island, off Tasmania's north-western corner, archaeologists have sunk trenches and discovered stone artefacts, charcoal and the remains of native mammals. Other caves have shown similar evidence of early human occupation. Caves found not long ago on the Franklin and Gordon rivers in south-western Tasmania, especially the huge Kutikina (formerly Fraser) Cave, reveal old campsites where people left behind large quantities of artefacts and the bones of animals they had hunted.

Other exciting discoveries about human life in ancient Australia have been made on the land's surface. In south-western New South Wales lie the dried-up lakes known as the Willandra Lakes. One of these freshwater lakes is Lake Mungo. Fragments of cooking hearths, animal bones and stone tools have been found on this lake's ancient shoreline. The site, however, has yielded something else—the skeletons of Aboriginal people once living there, including the skeleton of a young woman whose body was cremated and buried on the lake's edge about 25 000 years ago. From the evidence of nearby fossil residue it seems that she and her companions hunted marsupials such as rat-kangaroos, native cats and larger animals. Other food included emu eggs, small birds, shellfish and the golden perch—a fish of considerable size. The presence of bone awls and other tools indicates that Aborigines at Lake Mungo could have fashioned skin cloaks to ward off the cold. There in early times a small group of Aboriginal people with a distinct culture must have established a lakeside camp. Further digging has led to other finds: one highlight has been the discovery near the lake in 1974 of a man's skeleton, buried in a shallow grave about 30 000 years ago and with ochre scattered over his body. Deeper excavation in the area has disclosed more tools, hints of even earlier settlement.

Different branches of science help in investigating prehistory, the period before the written record. In 1968 the geomorphologist Dr Jim Bowler, from the Australian National University, recognised the fossil landscape of the Willandra Lakes and began the exploration of Lake Mungo's mysteries. Anatomists have examined the bones found there, while other scientists have analysed further remains. Estimating the age of the material discovered has been vital. Usually excavations expose progressively older remains as digging goes deeper, with the lowest layers

An archaeological digging site at Fromm's Landing, River Murray, South Australia

representing very old societies. But exactly how old? Techniques such as radiocarbon dating have helped to give reasonably accurate answers.

Radiocarbon, or Carbon 14, dating was developed after the identification in 1947 of Carbon 14 in natural substances. It measures the radioactive carbon present in once-living animal or plant matter, including shell and charcoal. Carbon 14 is lost at a constant rate over time, enabling laboratory testing of the age of this organic matter. Items like stone implements found with such material can be given an approximate age as well. The letters BP (Before the Present—that is, before 1950, when the technique was developed) are often placed after the dates determined. Scientists also use fluorine or uranium absorption analysis to help estimate the age of certain material. A recent technique—assessing the age of desert varnish on rock faces—provides a means of dating rock engravings (petroglyphs), some of which have been found to be almost 40 000 years old. Another ingenious technique, developed in Canberra, relies on extracting a sample of blood from ancient bone. Blood protein trapped in bone can survive almost unchanged, and can be tested by radiocarbon dating.

Two new techniques—measuring thermoluminescence (TL), by recording the energy released when material is heated, and optically-stimulated luminescence (OSL), by recording the energy released when material is irradiated with light—have produced remarkable results. These techniques, able to fix older dates than radiocarbon dating, have given an age of almost 60 000 years for stone tools and ochre from excavations in rock shelters in Arnhem Land. These excavations have thus produced traces of the earliest known human occupation in Australia, as well as indications of possibly the oldest art known anywhere. Similarities between the lifestyle of these early northern people in Australia and people in early South-East Asia have also been noticed, strengthening the probability of very early sea travel (possibly the earliest lengthy sea voyages ever made) from South-East Asia to Australia.

The range of dates across the continent shows that Aborigines have occupied Australia for hundreds of centuries. White people, in comparison, have been residents for only a moment in time. In Western Australia, at Devil's Lair at Augusta, bone tools, hearths and burnt animal bones more than 30 000 years old have been found, and near the upper Swan River there are signs of human activity almost 40 000 years before the present. In the north, the Arnhem Land discoveries help to confirm the presence 60 000 years ago of people resembling those in early Asia. Suggestions, though difficult to prove, have even been made that humans have occupied Australia for 100 000 years. From radiocarbon dating of traces of food and charcoal it is reasonably certain that people of Aboriginal type occupied much of the continent at least 30 000 years ago. Investigations of burials have also revealed other features of early Aboriginal life. Decorative material has been found, such as a necklace of Tasmanian devils' teeth on a man buried in western New South Wales. Glimpses of religious practices have come not only at Lake Mungo but at other burial places, including sites at Roonka Flat on the lower River Murray in South Australia and at Kow Swamp in Victoria. Aboriginal society in older Australia had an obvious spiritual focus, as well as a concern for physical survival in an often harsh environment.

The Origins of the Aboriginal People and Movement to Australia

To those seeking a scientific explanation of Aboriginal origins, it is most unlikely that the Aboriginal people originated in Australia, as an early theory once suggested. The ancestors of Aborigines probably lived in South-East Asia. *Homo sapiens*, the human type from which modern peoples have come, emerged and spread more than a million years ago in Africa, Europe and Asia. Human fossil remains and implements of stone and bone in Asia are much older than any found in Australia. Migration from Asia—corresponding with Aboriginal stories of voyaging across the seas—is the most likely explanation of how Australia was first settled.

Early migrants, lacking a land bridge as far as Australia, must have travelled partly by sea to reach the continent, like the modern 'boat people' who have arrived in small vessels to seek refuge. It seems certain that the first migrants, with no large sea-going craft, accomplished any necessary sea travel by simple means. Polynesians and Melanesians are known to have moved from island to island by canoe. Ancestors of the Aborigines, travelling at different times and in small family groups, could have used bark canoes or, more likely, rafts made from poles lashed together— Aborigines in modern times also have canoes and rafts.

Such frail craft could have been sufficient because conditions in the Australian region were then very different. Between 100 000 and 10 000 years ago—the latter part of the Pleistocene period in the earth's history—there were alternating periods of ice formation and warmer climate. During the ice periods (the glacial stages) much ocean water was taken up as ice, with ice sheets forming at the poles and the resulting lower ocean level exposing land previously submerged. When ice melted in the warmer periods, ocean levels rose, covering some of the exposed land again. Migration towards Australia would have been easier when more land was exposed and shorter sea journeys were possible. In the last ice period enough water would have been taken up not only to establish land bridges between former islands but to expose the Sunda Shelf in South-East Asia and the Sahul Shelf north of Australia. Today sixty metres of water covers the Sahul Shelf, but in the last ice period New Guinea was connected to Australia; to the south, Kangaroo Island and Tasmania

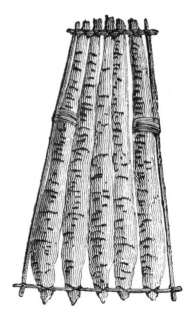

Mangrove logs lashed together to form a raft, Northern Australia, early nineteenth century

were part of the same continental land mass. Sea journeys
of from fifty to one hundred kilometres remained between
Asia and Australia, still difficult enough to cause many
people over the centuries to perish in attempts to cross by
raft or canoe. Probably some special factors, such as a
rising population and food shortages, forced people to
venture towards the Australian land mass from South-East
Asia; perhaps these led to the presence in Arnhem Land of
ancestors of the Aborigines about 60 000 years ago.

The New Land

Aborigines arriving in Australia more than 10 000 years
ago would have reached a land quite different from today.
Several stages of climatic change occurred in this last part
of the Pleistocene period. At one time there were glaciers
on the Great Dividing Range and in Tasmania. A higher
rainfall fell across the continent and much of it was clothed
in vegetation. Chains of lakes and rivers in areas now arid
were full of fish. Shellfish were common. Humans were
not alone in this more fertile landscape, sharing it with
creatures of curious form and sometimes giant size. The
largest was *Diprotodon*, a shambling, four-legged creature
with big toes turned at right angles. At about three metres
long, it resembled a hippopotamus. There was a large
kangaroo (*Procoptodon*) three metres tall, which could pull
down branches of trees; a giant wombat (*Phascolonus*); a
giant emu (*Genyornis*); and a marsupial lion (*Thylacoleo*),
with great slicing teeth capable of tearing its victims' flesh.
Among the other giant fauna (the *megafauna*) were tortoises
and koalas. In places such as Lake Eyre there were once
porpoises and crocodiles.
    These creatures have died out from the interior of the
country, leaving fascinating collections of bones to puzzle
science. Why did these animals die? What, for example,
caused the death of hundreds of *Diprotodons* at Lake
Callabonna in South Australia, where they apparently flayed
about in the boggy lake in a last desperate bid for survival
before the lake became their graveyard? Did Aborigines
play a role in their extinction? Or did climatic change cause
their end? It is known that Aborigines and the old fauna
existed at the same time. (Some Aboriginal stories may
actually refer to that now-extinct fauna.) By the evidence of
crushed and charred bones of the ancient animals, and
even blood on stone tools, it seems that the arrival of
Aborigines in Australia hastened the end of the megafauna.

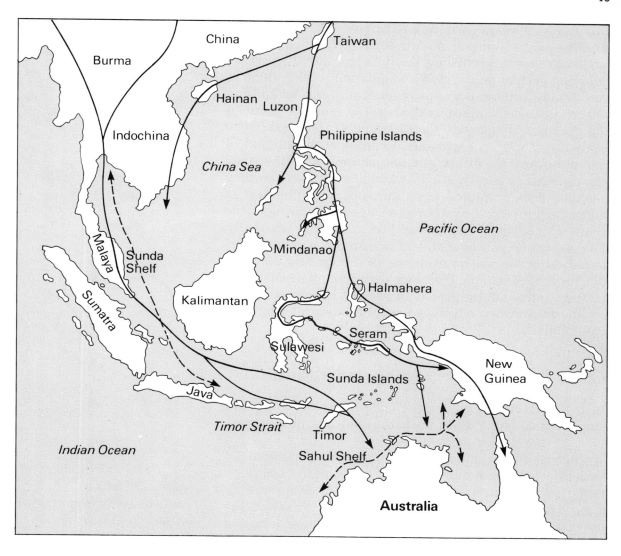

Possible migration routes to Australia in early times. Note the Sunda and Sahul shelfs, once exposed as land

Rather than living in an easy balance with nature, Aborigines were actively changing that balance.

Their most dynamic agent of change was fire. Early European navigators along Australia's coasts, such as Cook and Flinders, often saw smoke and fires ashore. Aborigines used fire extensively to burn the bush in patches at a time. Animals could be flushed out by this method and more easily killed. There was also another effect—fire destroyed the existing surface matter and allowed new shrubs and grass to grow, ideal for future hunting. The controlled burning over different sections of ground encouraged a better and more varied food supply. This method of burning has been called 'firestick farming'. Occurring yearly in some places, it seems to have been practised for thousands of years. A dating technique helps to confirm this: the analysis of pollen grain samples from cores taken at certain sites can provide a tiny window into the past. By counting ancient pollen grains at different levels, scientists can detect earlier patterns of vegetation. Cores taken from the bed of Lake George near Canberra have shown, through the presence of charcoal, that between 125 000 and 50 000 years ago a sudden expansion occurred in the amount of fire in the area; the existing casuarina forest was destroyed and replaced by eucalypts and wattles. Ancient land burning has also been identified from the Atherton Tableland in north Queensland. Did Aborigines cause this firing of the country? If so, their fires changed the country dramatically. The vegetation was altered, and in turn other living things increased or decreased in numbers. Firing was not only practised in Australia, for other early people used fire in hunting and to aid the growth of pasture. Like those people in other continents, Aborigines were actively altering their environment.

Other Ideas about Origins and Migration

In 1845 Edward John Eyre, the famous explorer and close student of Aboriginal life, made the following observation:

The Aborigines of Australia . . . present a striking similarity to each other in physical appearance and structure; and also in their general character, habits, and pursuits. Any difference that is found to exist is only the consequence of local circumstances or influences, and such as might naturally be expected to be met with among a people spread over such an immense extent of country.[1]

Despite the similarity reported by Eyre, it has been suggested that Aborigines in Australia stem from the migrations of different groups. Difference, rather than similarity, has been the focus of investigation. Some years ago J.B. Birdsell suggested that there must have been three distinct movements of Asian people to Australia. He identified differences in Aboriginal people living along the River Murray, in Arnhem Land and in north-eastern Queensland. An even greater difference was noted between mainland Aborigines and those in Tasmania: the Tasmanians, with their simpler living style and different appearance, could have come from Melanesia, drifting by raft or canoe

An artist's impression of what a Diprotodon probably looked like, based on skeletal discoveries, especially near Lake Callabonna

Aborigines on a log raft, Northern Australia, early nineteenth century

and chancing upon Tasmania, as the Maoris must have found New Zealand.

New discoveries and ideas have overthrown such older theories. Again, differences have been emphasised, this time in the important fossil skulls found at various sites. A significant group of skulls has been discovered at Kow Swamp in northern Victoria. These Aborigines, living about 8 000 to 15 000 years ago, had a more rugged appearance, with stronger jaws and a flat, receding forehead. Similar finds have been made elsewhere, including one at Willandra Lakes. At Lake Mungo and in other places, however, the early skeletons are of a more finely featured people, of more modern appearance.

Do these discoveries confirm that different types of people arrived in Australia in earlier times? Or did people of only one type come, gradually developing different characteristics in separate parts of the continent? Answers vary. Fossil remains show differences among early Aborigines, as revealed by the discovery of the skeleton of a Willandra Lakes man of more rugged appearance near the remains of the finely-featured Lake Mungo people. People of two rather different types might have come to Australia, perhaps living alongside each other for 30 000 years or more, with modern Aborigines being descended from both groups. Yet signs of major difference, such as in material culture, language or social customs, have not been found, making it doubtful whether the migrations were of very different peoples.

Ideas about the pattern and density of settlement in earlier times are also being revised. Aborigines may once have been more numerous in coastal areas than in the arid centre of the continent. The Lake Mungo people were living in a coastal manner on the lake's edge more than 30 000 years ago. At other sites along Australia's ancient coasts there are frequent traces of early Aboriginal occupation. (Many former camping-places now almost certainly lie submerged off the coasts.) But the recent discoveries of artefacts and ochre dating beyond 20 000 years in central Australia, together with material objects at other inland sites, indicate that Aborigines did not ignore drier places in early times.

The Tasmanians

Theories about the origins of Australia's Aborigines need to explain the arrival of Aborigines in Tasmania, their isolation for up to 12 000 years and their differences from mainland Aborigines. The differences have often been stressed. Before European settlement the Tasmanian Aborigines lived as nine distinct groups, with five different languages. They kept to a simpler level of stone tool industry than the mainlanders, with no hafted and ground-edge axes. They had no boomerangs, spear-throwers or shields; they used spears and clubs and threw stones without the aid of a sling. Stone choppers and scrapers were their chief implements. Deposits of stone fragments and heaps of shells are the main indications of their former life, but they left some fine examples of basketwork. They used neither nets nor fish-hooks (they originally ate fish, but later avoided it). Their society has often been pictured as less developed than on the mainland, but they proved very effective in satisfying a wide range of needs.

New information about the early Tasmanian Aborigines, whose descendants live in Tasmania today, has come steadily

Tasmanian Aborigines and their canoes, near Schouten Island. (A French engraving, published in 1807)

Hand axes formerly used by Tasmanian Aborigines

in the last few years. Much has been learned by excavating in caves, favourite places for early inhabitants in the once-icy climate. Researchers now reject the early view that Tasmania's Aborigines arrived by sea from Melanesia—there is, for example, no evidence of their use of ocean-going craft either in very early or more recent times. Nor is it likely that the Tasmanians were the very first arrivals on the Australian mainland and were later gradually forced southwards into Tasmania by later immigrants. The Aboriginal occupation of Tasmania has nevertheless been traced back to over 30 000 years. The arrival of Aborigines in Tasmania was clearly effected through the use of the early land bridge from the mainland. In the glacial time, when the world entered a colder phase and ocean water was taken up as ice, Bass Strait became exposed land. Mainland Aborigines could then move by land to the south, reaching Tasmania and places such as Cave Bay Cave. In some caves there remain hand outlines stencilled in ochre, examples of their early art. At the end of the last ice age the waters rose again, so that about 12 000 years ago Tasmania was once more becoming separated from the mainland. The land route to Tasmania was closed, isolating the people there. The dingo, which arrived in Australia about 4 000 years ago, thus could not reach the island. In isolation Tasmania's Aborigines adapted to often severe conditions, surviving with great fortitude and skill until a hostile European culture finally overwhelmed their traditional life.

Woureddy, a Tasmanian Aborigine of the 1830s

The Population

Engraved boulders, Mount Cameron West, Tasmania

Further questions have often been asked about traditional Aboriginal societies before European colonisation began in 1788. What was the total size of the population, and how was it distributed across Australia? Various answers have been given, but the size and distribution of the population obviously altered greatly as the climate varied over the centuries. Changing sea levels during and after the last ice age affected land areas and food supplies. Vegetation and animal numbers fluctuated. Aborigines themselves, by firing the land and harvesting its resources, continued their active role in changing the environment. After the last ice age the sea settled near its modern level; coastal rainforests developed in the north and fertile tracts appeared in the south. The Aboriginal population seems to have increased steadily in many of these favourable places, as indicated by the survival of large shellfish middens and many stone tools of fairly recent origin. The dry interior was more sparsely settled. Yet Aborigines could survive in the harsher areas, for they had developed the technology, the knowledge of their environment and the social relationships to do so. Aboriginal society had not been static over the centuries. Aborigines showed themselves able to adapt continuously to life on the Australian continent.

Because Aborigines were not counted in the official Australian censuses before 1971, their total population before that date can only be estimated. A figure of about 300 000 for the whole of Australia in 1788 has often been accepted. An anthropologist supplied this figure in 1930, when Aboriginal numbers had declined alarmingly. He examined the available evidence to calculate how many people could have been supported in 1788 in different parts of the country. Today, with evidence that higher numbers once lived in some areas and that the food supply was probably adequate, this estimate has been increased beyond 300 000 to more than double that figure.

Contact with Other Peoples

Once the Australian continent had taken something like its present form, the surrounding seas became a barrier to contact between Aborigines and people beyond the continent. Aborigines had no need to explore and travel the seas. But at certain times people from other lands did so. In the two centuries before 1788 European navigators, in particular those from Holland and England, visited Australian waters. Chinese explorers might have made similar journeys earlier. The closest contacts, however, came from Papuan people across Torres Strait, and from Indonesian people who visited Australia's northern shores.

The Papuans had a strong impact in the Cape York area. Apart from the physical mixing of Papuan and Aboriginal peoples, the Papuan cultural influence extended far down Cape York Peninsula. Different languages were found close together: Papuan and Aboriginal language groups survive today on separate Torres Strait islands. Agriculture, practised in some Torres Strait islands and in Papua New Guinea, did not spread to the mainland at Cape York, but the people there did adopt the dugout canoe, with its outriggers, as well as other elements of the life of their northern neighbours. Torres Strait Islanders have retained close ties with mainland people. (Today the term 'Aborigines' is usually taken to include them, though 'Aborigines and Torres Strait Islanders' is also frequently used.) Papuan culture also had an impact in Arnhem Land, where painted graveposts and ornamental masks were introduced. In return, Papuans acquired spears, spear-throwers and ornaments from Aborigines as part of the exchange in goods and ideas across Torres Strait.

The Indonesians who visited the northern shores of Australia were Bugis and Macassan seamen. From at least the eighteenth century until early this century they made regular journeys south-eastwards. Their main purpose was to dive for trepang (sea-slug). Blown in their praus (sailing boats with outriggers) by the monsoon winds, these voyagers reached Australia at Arnhem Land, Groote Eylandt and the north-western coast of Western Australia. There they gathered trepang and shell until the south-easterlies came, after which they abandoned their coastal camps for the voyage home.

The English navigators Matthew Flinders and Phillip Parker King, exploring independently along Australia's northern coast in the early nineteenth century, met these seamen. King recorded that their provisions consisted chiefly of rice and coconuts, and that they carried their water in joints of bamboo. They had an important influence on the Aborigines, introducing iron for fish-hooks and knives to Arnhem Land, and leaving traces of their contact in art and language. They introduced the dugout canoe, or *lippa-lippa*, to the Aboriginal people there, who previously used only bark canoes. Arnhem Land Aborigines also travelled on

Macassan praus at Raffles Bay, Northern Territory, in 1839

the praus to Macassar. Aborigines acquired the practice of smoking from these northern visitors—men, women and children in Arnhem Land passed long wooden pipes from person to person. The significant effects of all this contact was reflected in the social and ceremonial life of the Aborigines in the area, especially in song cycles, dance and language. Relics of the Indonesian presence (such as stone hearths and pottery) have lingered at their former coastal camps, while the sites themselves are often obvious by the appearance of tamarind trees growing from fruit brought by the Macassans. But the contact between the peoples remained coastal—the northerners, enjoying sometimes friendly but at other times unfriendly relations with the local Aboriginal groups, did not move inland.

Apart from the Papuan and Indonesian influences in the recent period, people from nearby lands undertook little travel towards Australia and made no permanent settlement in it. In 1888 a white explorer familiar with Australia's environment suggested a reason:

... the force of nature was against it; the new land of the south held forth no inducements even for the pirate or marauder. In the hand to mouth struggle for existence, not even a supply of food would be found in a ransacked camp; no land seen tempting settlement by its luxuriant vegetation and produce. The visitors of the straits scorned the inhospitable coast, and returned north.[2]

This left the Aboriginal people as sole occupants of the Australian continent before 1788. By then their achievements were notable. Clearly Aborigines must have been among the first in very early times to make ocean voyages and settle in a new land. They survived for thousands of

Macassan trepanging camp at Raffles Bay, 1839. Note the huts, cauldrons and praus

years in an often severe environment, without needing to adopt agriculture or use metals. Their technology and social organisation were effective. Their art, enriched by the use of ochre, was amongst the world's oldest, as was their development of religious beliefs, demonstrated in the Lake Mungo burial of more than 30 000 years ago.

The Aboriginal people probably had the oldest known culture when European settlement began in 1788. European colonists, however, when describing Aboriginal culture as 'primitive' and 'stone-age' and referring to the lack of written languages, showed little understanding of the complexity of Aboriginal life. As for the Aboriginal migration to Australia, the prehistorian Rhys Jones has made the following observation:

The human colonisation of Australia was one of the great events in history. It added a continent to the human domain and it occurred as one of the key events in the global expansion of modern sapient man.[3]

Note: For further study relating to this chapter, see the Reading List at the end of the book. Josephine Flood's books, Archaeology of the Dreamtime (rev. edn 1995) and The Riches of Ancient Australia (rev. edn 1993), are especially useful.

1 Eyre, E.J. Journals of Expeditions of Discovery into Central Australia . . . T. and W. Boone, London, 1845, vol. 2, p. 206.
2 Favenc, E. The History of Australian Exploration from 1788 to 1888, Turner and Henderson, Sydney, 1888, p. 385.
3 Rhys Jones, in Hardy, J. and Frost, A. (eds) Studies from Terra Australis to Australia, Australian Academy of the Humanities, Canberra, 1989, p. 11.

MATERIAL LIFE IN TRADITIONAL SOCIETY

White colonisation from 1788 shattered the Aborigines' sole occupation of Australia. The Aboriginal people, settlers in the continent for at least 30 000 years, found their land being wrenched away from them. The process was sometimes violent, and white settlers made little effort to justify what they were doing. When they bothered to give reasons, they talked about Australia being an empty continent, about Aborigines apparently not owning land, and about whites having a superior culture which ought to be spread among 'uncivilised' peoples. But whites made little effort to find out what Aboriginal life was really like. Instead, Aboriginal life was quickly branded as primitive: features of it were soon described as quaint or hostile, and Aborigines were often simply condemned as a people of boomerangs, 'corroborees' and spears.

Such judgments were hasty and inaccurate. Aborigines had developed a society that was well organised and on a much higher level than most white people realised. It also suffered much less from disease. Nor had traditional Aboriginal society been unchanging since ancient times, as whites often thought. The impact of white invasion, however, brought change on a scale not known before. Traditional Aboriginal society was broken down rapidly as white settlement occurred, especially in coastal districts; inland, chiefly in drier and remote districts, it survived much longer in its original form. Indeed, traditional Aboriginal society did not die out completely—today Aborigines in rural and urban Australia retain many elements of the traditional way of life and often try to revive lost features of it. But a clearer understanding of traditional society comes from looking not at the present but at the past—at the period before so much destruction of Aboriginal life, and lives, took place. This

An Aboriginal man hunting in the Fraser Range, Western Australia, late in the nineteenth century

and the next chapter in this book are thus written in the past tense, to describe Aborigines and their traditional society before the era of overwhelming change began.

The People

In their traditional society Aborigines, a people of brown skin pigment and with hair that was usually dark brown or black, varied little in appearance throughout the continent. They had adapted well to the severe Australian environment. Their physique was suited to the exertions of hunting and gathering food. Younger Aborigines in particular were erect, long-limbed and agile. An observer who knew Northern Territory Aborigines well was impressed by their grace of movement, and remarked:

Have you ever seen the desert man on the move? Chest thrown out and head back, he does not appear to walk but glides over the ground with springing stride; no fuss, no worry, the same pace, mile after mile, singing as he goes to make the distant object come nearer to him.[1]

This kind of graceful movement was noted, too, in Aboriginal women, who while travelling could carry water in bark containers on their heads without spilling it, or piles of firewood in the same fashion.

Aborigines displayed the same easy, assured movement in other activities demanding strenuous effort, such as stalking game, tree climbing and swimming. In climbing trees, for example, the Aborigines were expert. They cut notches to assist their foothold, used a strong piece of vine or rope to hoist themselves, or merely pulled and levered their bodies up the butt with hands and feet. (They also used the other method of reaching a treetop—lighting a fire around the base of the trunk to enable the flames to topple the tree.)

An Aboriginal drawing of a kangaroo hunt in the nineteenth century

Aborigines also had good eyesight, suffering less from short-sightedness than Europeans, though their keen perception of objects was above all a matter of knowing what to look for. Thus an Aborigine would observe bubbles of air or pieces of nibbled seaweed rising to the water's surface, indicating perhaps a crocodile or dugong beneath. Eye disease, however, was common among Aborigines, in a land where the effects of dust and flies were severe.

Adapting to the Climate

Part of the Aborigines' success in surviving in the Australian environment came from their ability to cope with extremes of temperature. In very hot weather they took care to conserve energy, travelling by night if necessary. A Central Australian Aborigine described how his people journeyed in such weather:

. . . when Aborigines are forced to travel in summer over long, dry stages, they do not set out on their journey until nightfall. Before leaving the last waterhole, they drink as much as possible, then keep going until a little after sunrise. When the day starts to warm up, the Aborigines dig a hole under a tree until they reach the cool sand. Then they put a rough shelter over the top, reduce their skin temperature by throwing sand over their bodies, bury themselves up to the neck, and remain covered until the cool of the evening allows them to continue their way.[2]

In cold weather Aborigines would often sleep between fires at night—though it might bring the risk of rolling on to hot embers. The explorer Captain S.A. White recorded that the Aborigines would laugh at whites, who when camping made large fires that scorched one side of the body without warming the other. Captain White noted that Aborigines would 'sleep upon the ground in a row, hollowing out a place for their hips to rest in. A small fire is kept going on either side, and when it dies down the cold awakens them, and they put on fresh fuel. They do not really sleep for any time, just dozing off for a little while, and awaken with a start in case the fires are out.'[3]

Generally Aborigines preferred to live and sleep in the open, though on rainy or windy days they could erect a

A woman wearing a skin rug, near Lake Alexandrina, South Australia, probably about 1900. Note how the child was carried

hut or windbreak, or if travelling carry burning sticks to
provide warmth for their bodies. Grease could be
smeared over the skin to ward off the cold. In some parts
of Australia, especially in the south, Aborigines wore
possum, wallaby or kangaroo skin rugs, the result of
much careful treatment of skins and sewing them
together.

Aboriginal huts were known by a variety of names,
such as *mia-mia, wiltja, wurley* and *gunyah*, and were ideal-
ly suited to the needs of the people. They could be
erected in a very short time from materials near at hand,
and were surprisingly strong and resistant to wind, rain
and dust. A small fire at the entrance gave warmth and
deterred mosquitoes, while the dark interior discouraged
flies. Bark, branches and grass were the materials commonly used. A hut usually had a circular base, with a
roof fastened at a peak or left rounded. In the wet season
in Arnhem Land, Aborigines built a bark-covered plat-
form, below which a fire burned to ward off insects. In
some places, where people made seasonal camps, huts
were sturdier and could be insulated with a layer of
leaves, mud, seaweed, animal skins or sand. Rock shelters provided a natural sleeping place in many areas.

*A man of the Milmenrura
people, South Australia, in
the 1840s, wearing a
seaweed cloak*

*Aborigines at their wiltja
in the Everard Range,
South Australia, as
photographed on the Elder
Expedition, 1891–92*

A hut made of fan palm leaves, North Queensland

The Search for Water

Finding water often took much knowledge and skill. Of course water from rivers and waterholes might be readily available, but in drier parts the search for water was less easily solved. Water might then have to be obtained from the roots and stems of trees such as the mallee, the mulga, the kurrajong, the needlebush and the desert oak. It might also be found stored in the hollow of a tree, notably the bottle-shaped baobab tree. The explorer David Lindsay saw an Aboriginal woman suck water from a cavity in a tree through tubes of bark. She had found the water after noticing small ants going in and out of a hole in a fork of the tree. Often Aborigines were guided to water by the presence of finches, pigeons or parrots. Aborigines could also get water from rockholes and carefully concealed wells, which they often enlarged but kept secret from other groups. They also took care to cover the mouth of a well to prevent animals from drinking or fouling the water.

The explorers Ludwig Leichhardt and Ernest Giles noticed another means by which Aborigines conserved water—using wooden shovels to build small dams. Occasionally, while travelling, Aborigines also carried water in a skin bag or wooden vessel, or even, as in southern South Australia, in a human skull container (frequently the skull of a deceased relative).

Often in dry areas Aborigines would simply rely on getting water from dew-laden grass, wiping or shaking the grass over a wooden vessel known as a *coolamon* or *pitchi*. A more unusual, but still effective, method in these

areas was to dig beneath the surface of a claypan and find a species of frog patiently awaiting the end of a drought. The frog had stored water in its body to tide it over the drought, and the water was perfectly fresh and drinkable.

The key to the water quest in drier areas was detailed knowledge of the country. This knowledge was jealously guarded. W.E. Harney, who knew the Aborigines well, records:

There is nothing mysterious about it, just tradition handed on from mother to daughter and father to son, but with that tradition is a rigid law—none may disclose the secret watering-paces of the tribe. To do so is to betray the people; therefore the native who divulges the secret is doomed to death. Observing this law they never camp near the water. No road leads to these places. Each person must take a different route and all tracks must be erased.[4]

To the Aborigines, living in a drought-prone continent, water was life.

Wailbri boys drinking from a rockhole, Northern Territory

A skin for carrying water. These were made from possum, wallaby or kangaroo skin, with the fur turned inside and the holes tied

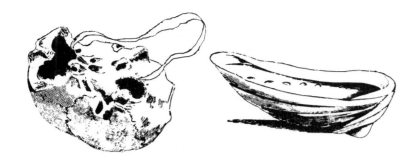

Drinking vessels: a skull with holes stopped up with gum, and a shell

A few other beverages, such as wild honey, were available. Sweet drinks could be made by soaking nectar-laden flowers in water, or by adding wild-bee's honey to water. It is said that in northern Australia a drink was made by soaking the fruit of the pandanus palm; if the liquid fermented it produced a mildly intoxicating substance to be drunk on festive occasions. In south-western Australia another drink, made by soaking grasstree cones, had a similar effect. Water, however, remained the universal drink, and when drought pressed sorely and water was unobtainable there was scarcely any substitute.

The Search for Food

The search for food could also demand skill and perseverance. Once again Aborigines showed their close knowledge of the environment, acute powers of observation, and ingenuity in attaining their goal. Considerable differences existed throughout the continent in the type and quantity of food available, but Aborigines became adept at hunting and food gathering in all kinds of conditions. Along the coasts they were proficient in winning food from the sea. Inland they were expert hunters of game. Along rivers and streams away from the coast the arts of fishing were again employed, while in hilly or mountainous country, in rainforest or the vast inland desert, Aborigines had other skilful means of obtaining food.

Different methods of finding food led to different forms of daily life. Hunters and gatherers in the interior often had to move widely to find food in the arid surroundings, and had few possessions to burden them as they searched. But near the sea and along the bigger inland rivers (especially in the Murray-Darling basin, where the

I am giving no false picture of the reality. So long had the drought continued, that the vegetable kingdom was almost annihilated, and minor vegetation had disappeared. In the creeks, weeds had grown and withered, and grown again; and young saplings were now rising in their beds, nourished by the moisture that still remained; but the largest forest trees were drooping, and many were dead. The emus, with out-stretched necks, gasping for breath, searched the channels of the rivers for water, in vain; and the native dog, so thin that it could hardly walk, seemed to implore some merciful hand to despatch it. How the natives subsisted it was difficult to say, but there was no doubt of the scarcity of food among them.
Charles Sturt: *Two Expeditions into the Interior of Southern Australia* . . ., London, 1833, Vol. 1, p. 145.

Captain Sturt's description of drought in the interior of New South Wales in 1829

food supply could support a comparatively large population) it was possible to lead a much more settled existence. Here Aborigines had more equipment, such as nets, fishing lines and canoes. But for women and children methods of food-gathering did not vary much— their task was to forage for such things as plant food, birds' eggs, small mammals, lizards, edible grubs and even honey. Moreover they often had greater success in finding food than the men, who could return empty-handed from a long day's hunting. While the men's hunting is often considered the adventurous and typical way in which food was obtained, the women in fact were the chief food-suppliers among the Aboriginal people. Gathering rather than hunting—and women rather than men—supported most Aboriginal groups.

The honey ant

Food gathering was usually a matter for the small local groups of Aborigines. Each sex and age group had tasks to perform. Food was shared according to rules. The time and energy needed to gather food varied with the conditions, but it usually left plenty of time for leisure. Agriculture was not practised, and only occasionally did some Aboriginal groups store food. In northern Queensland palm nuts and kernels were stored for months, and turtle eggs and birds' eggs were pulped and kept; in Central Australia Aborigines dried and preserved strips of kangaroo meat;[5] along Australia's southern coast whale meat was sometimes stored. But food was normally procured only for immediate needs. It was a tribute to Aboriginal skills that the people could exist fairly easily without the larders and barns so necessary in other societies.

Food from the Sea

At the coast Aboriginal groups obtained a variety of seafood, often allowing them to live more easily than Aborigines elsewhere. In shallow water fish were caught in traps or driven into hand-sewn nets. Other methods of catching fish included spearing them from above or below the surface and using a hook and line. Quite large fish were also caught—it was not uncommon for Aborigines to feast on mulloway, dolphin or shark, or even a stranded whale. In northern Australia canoes were often used in fishing. Aborigines would throw harpoons attached to a long cord line, occasionally spearing a turtle

or dugong by this means; if the desperate victim did not succeed in breaking free, a large amount of food could be won.

Aborigines on the North Queensland coast had a remarkable way of getting such a prize. A sucker fish—a species which fastens itself to a turtle or dugong by a disc above its head—was caught and a line was fastened to it. Then, sighting their prey from a canoe, the Aborigines would cast the sucker fish towards it. After the sucker attached itself to the dugong or turtle, a tense struggle would begin, often ending with the animal being drawn near the canoe and harpooned. The task demanded great skill. One observer declared:

How they accomplish the feat of securing a turtle that may weigh a couple of hundredweight from a frail bark canoe, in which a white man can scarcely sit and preserve his balance, is astonishing. In a lively sea the blacks sit back, tilting up the stem to meet the coming wave, and then put their weight

Fishing with nets in the sea at Rapid Bay, South Australia, in the 1840s

Fishing from a canoe, as depicted by an Aboriginal artist in the nineteenth century

forward to ease it down, paddling, manoeuvring with the line
and baling all the time. The mere paddling about in the canoe
is a feat beyond the dexterity of an ordinary man.[6]

In North Queensland, too, Aborigines showed their ingenuity in fishing by constructing tidal fish traps on
Hinchinbrook Island.

Other seafood at the coast included crabs, crayfish and
many varieties of shellfish. Elsewhere at the coast great
middens (mounds of shells) have been found, reminders
of the Aboriginal liking for, and occasional reliance on,
this seafood. An observer records that a sand midden on
the west coast of Tasmania bore abundant traces of con-
tinuous Aboriginal feasting on shellfish, with occasional
banquets on the carcases of sea-leopards, seals, whales
and other marine creatures cast ashore.[7]

Coast-dwellers, of course, also obtained food from
sources other than the water itself. Tasmanians used their
canoes to visit islands (muttonbird eggs, for example,
could be found at Bruny Island), and mainland Aborigines also journeyed to small islands offshore. Birds and
birds' eggs, an occasional seal or dugong, plant food and
small mammals—all were added to the coast-dwellers'
diet. But the sea itself gave a wonderful harvest, so that
it was seldom necessary to travel far from it. The coastal
campsites, each used fairly regularly, and the rather small
local territories around them were centres of Aboriginal
life at the land's edge. At the coast there were also tidal
areas and lakes (as in Arnhem Land and at the Coorong

*A fish-hook from
Rockingham Bay,
Queensland. The hook is
made from shell*

*Present-day remains of an
old midden, Robe, South
Australia*

in South Australia) where nature's harvest was particularly bountiful.

Freshwater Food

Along inland rivers and streams Aborigines usually had a plentiful food supply, not only in the form of shellfish but also waterfowl, fish, tortoise and platypus. The Aborigines paid careful attention to weirs, nets and traps which they set up in these waterways. The best known and largest of the fish traps were built on the Barwon River at Brewarrina in New South Wales. Here stone pens trapped fish when the river level was falling. Elsewhere the falling water level was also helpful—in Arnhem Land it allowed Aborigines to spear the fine barramundi as billabongs dried up. Another method was simply to poison the water by soaking poisonous leaves, bark or fruit in it, so that fish could be readily gathered.

The abundant food along the rivers allowed many Aborigines to live there. The lands along the River Murray were greatly favoured, as the explorer Captain Sturt found on his journey down that river. To many

Women fishing for freshwater crayfish in the River Murray (mid-nineteenth century, S.T. Gill)

people, Aborigines in traditional society have usually
been thought of as essentially hunters of land animals,
but they also secured much food from fresh water and
the sea. In this they were versatile and skilful, as their
talents in eel fishing revealed. Eels, highly valued, were
common along the coast and several inland waterways,
and were captured by various means. Often they were
simply speared, but in North Queensland worms were
skewered along a bobbing cane as a lure. In south-eastern
New South Wales bark soaked in water was found to
stun them. In Western Victoria a clever system of
drainage channels was devised to trap the eels in their
seasonal movement. In this district an early white settler
described fishing techniques on a river's swampy
margins:

At these places we found many low sod banks extending
across the shallow branches of the river, with apertures at
intervals, in which were placed long, narrow, circular nets (like
a large stocking) made of rush-work.[8]

The eel traps and associated structures in Western
Victoria were engineering achievements of an astonishing
kind. They guaranteed a large food supply, enabling
Aborigines there to live in a very settled fashion. A village
of more than a hundred stone houses has been discovered at Lake Condah. Hundreds of Aborigines would
gather each year at Lake Bolac, south of Ararat, to work
its eel traps. Large camps were made and meetings held.
Details about this and similar sites suggest that Aborigines skilfully managed, or 'farmed', the eel supply. In
Queensland there was also a trade in dried eels.

Hunting Game

Aborigines were highly proficient as hunters on land.
Men and older boys normally undertook the hunt for
larger animals such as kangaroos. This could be arduous,
for native animals were often scarce and shy. In lean
times it could take more than a day to track and kill a
kangaroo or wallaby. It was vital to know the habits of
the game being hunted, and vital to employ the skills of
stealthy movement and patient observation. These skills
were well described by an early writer:

*Hunting emus
(mid-nineteenth century,
S.T. Gill)*

As he walks through the bush, his step is light, elastic, and noiseless; every track on the earth catches his keen eye; a leaf or fragment of a stick turned, or a blade of grass recently bent by the tread of one of the lower animals, instantly arrests his attention; in fact, nothing escapes his quick and powerful sight on the ground, in the trees, or in the distance, which may supply him with a meal or warn him of danger.[9]

Camouflage and imitation were also employed when hunting. Bushes, grass and animal skins could be carried or worn, while the smell of the human body could be disguised by plastering the skin with mud. A spear might be dragged between the toes; the movements of animals could be imitated as the hunter followed the quarry. Family members would often help to find and surround the game, which was driven towards the spear-thrower or flushed out with fire. In the kill, the Aborigine relied on a keen eye and a strong arm. The spear was the weapon most often used, and it was thrown with great accuracy. The hunter could also bring down a bird with a quickly thrown club or stone.

Animals, like fish, were often taken in nets, placed along pathways. Another method was to dig a large pit on an animal track and conceal it beneath branches. Game such as wombats and echidnas usually had to be dug from their burrows. Tree-dwellers such as possums and flying foxes were pulled or smoked out of their hollows, or knocked from the branches with a boomerang. Waterfowl could be taken by an underwater swimmer

A snare to catch small animals

Cord mesh of a kangaroo net

breathing through a reed and pulling the birds below the surface. Major Mitchell, the explorer, witnessed another well-known method—frightening birds into a net suspended across a waterway. Snares, nooses, decoys and brush fences were further aids in the taking of game.

A hunting party, drawn by Yertabrida Solomon, an Aborigine from the Coorong, South Australia, and published in 1879

Seeking Other Food

The search for other sources of food was less spectacular, though persistent. Aborigines in local areas often relied on a single kind of food, such as seed food in Central Australia, for their basic diet, but a varied food supply was usually available. The general diet in traditional Aboriginal society seems to have been adequate and nutritious, often requiring only a few hours a day to collect it. The task thus left ample time for leisure. Food gathering, however, demanded sharp eyes and patience. Aboriginal women played a vital role by collecting plant food, which was of many kinds. Aborigines knew the natural world intimately and used dozens of its plants for food. Generally leaves, berries, roots, stems, nuts and other parts of a number of trees, bushes and smaller plants were collected. Items were prepared and eaten in different ways. Berries were eaten raw and seeds ground into a paste, while other foods were baked, pounded or soaked. Soaking in water was commonly done to remove poisonous substances found in several native plants. In places such as Central Australia, where game was often

Wood grubs in a metal coolamon, Ernabella country, South Australia. Metal and other materials of European origin were quickly adopted by Aborigines in traditional society

scarce, plant food was relied on. In northern Australia there was usually a wider variety of this type of food, though food such as yam tubers, which women probed for with their digging-sticks, was found in colder as well as tropical areas.

Several kinds of insect life, such as white ants, larval grubs and wasps, were also gathered. The wood grub was keenly sought, but took skill to find it. This grub lived in the roots of bushes or the trunks of trees, and had to be detected by patient testing of the roots or by sharp observation of the bark. Occasionally the sound of the grub inside the bark would indicate its presence. Once found, the grub could be withdrawn from its hole by means of a hooked twig and then lightly cooked. Its flavour has been likened to that of scrambled egg, slightly sweetened, or even butter. To Aborigines, wood grubs (often called witchetty grubs in inland areas) were an important part of their diet, providing good nourishment.

Sometimes the food search led to delicacies such as swan or emu eggs, freshwater crayfish, goannas, the honeycomb ('sugar bag') of the native bee, or the sweet substances produced by smaller insects. Sometimes, too, certain foods (like the eels mentioned earlier) were abundant, and neighbouring groups were invited to share the harvest. Thus in south-eastern Queensland many Aborigines assembled at the annual ripening of the Bunya Bunya pine cones to feast on the seeds. Another annual summer feast occurred in south-eastern Australia: Aborigines from neighbouring groups congregated in the Australian Alps to collect and roast Bogong moths migrating into the highlands. Hundreds of Aborigines feasted on the nutritious moths. This occasion was not solely a food festival: camps were carefully organised; social arrangements, including marriages, were made; goods and ceremonies were traded.

Though they would eat a wide variety of foods, for sacred reasons individual Aborigines often observed certain food restrictions, or 'taboos'. Tasmanian Aborigines, for example, would not eat fish other than shellfish, and wallabies were taboo to many of them. In Gippsland uninitiated Aborigines were not allowed to eat female animals except the wombat. Some foods were taboo for Aborigines at certain stages, or for the whole, of their lives. In effect these taboos amounted to conservation laws protecting game which would otherwise be hunted. Even great hunger might not result in these sacred restrictions being broken.

Knowledge of the environment and skill in using its resources enabled Aborigines to survive quite well in areas where Europeans could soon perish. Medical tests of Aborigines living in traditional societies confirmed this. A white medical doctor noted:

We have encountered Pintubi, members of a nomadic Western Desert tribe, immediately after they had completed a two-hundred-mile trek across apparently barren desert where the only possible food was little more than lizards and snakes. These people were hard, lean and fit and our studies of their blood showed no deficiencies whatever.[10]

Occasionally conditions bore hard on the Aboriginal people. Hunger could force an Aboriginal man to tighten the hair belt around his waist, and thirst could make him cover his stomach with earth. Extended droughts could even lead to death. But the Aborigines' ability not only to find enough food for a balanced diet but to have plenty of time for leisure and other activities was a tribute to their resourcefulness. Aborigines in fact could support themselves in higher numbers in drier parts of the continent than Europeans could do in later times—and with much less damage to the natural environment.

Stimulants

In general Aborigines in traditional society were unacquainted with intoxicants, and used narcotic substances
only to a limited degree. Apart from the habit of smoking
introduced by the Macassans, Aborigines chewed the
dried and powdered leaves of the wild tobacco bush
(*Nicotiana*), which contained very small amounts of
nicotine. Another practice widely known in Central
Australia was the chewing of *pituri*—the dried stems and
leaves of a shrub of the *Duboisia* species. This practice,
which was a regular habit among men, women and occasionally children across a wide inland area, gave a
stimulating effect from the nicotine released, especially
when burnt acacia ash was added. The source of the best
pituri, and the recipe for treating it, was kept a close
secret, but eager traders brought the substance from
south-western Queensland to other groups. *Pituri* also
had another use: it was placed in waterholes from which
an emu was likely to drink, causing the bird to become
drunk and an easy prey to the hunter. An observer
described the shrub and the vigorous trade in its product:

> The plant has the form of a small, stiff shrub with a number of
> straight stems, from four to six feet high, carrying yellow
> flowers and hard, narrow leaves. The leaves and little twigs
> are gathered . . . and packed tightly into bags of woven
> fur-string . . . These bags are traded for hundreds of miles,
> principally along an old trade route, passing from the north
> across the interior of Queensland and New South Wales, right
> to the south of Lake Eyre, shields, boomerangs, spears and
> other articles being traded back in return for them.[11]

*A wild tobacco bush,
growing in the Birksgate
Range, South Australia,
near the Western
Australian border, late
nineteenth century*

Camps

Aborigines in traditional society were not a solitary
people. They spent much of their time in groups, mostly
in small family parties; occasionally they would gather in
larger numbers, of perhaps dozens or even hundreds of
people, for special purposes. In daily life different
campsites in a local territory would be used, according to
food and other requirements. Some sites near available
water were occupied frequently. Often the preparation
and cooking of food was a central task in the camps, but

they were also centres of social life, including child rearing and leisure activities. (Aborigines did not observe the sharp distinction between 'leisure' and 'work' that Europeans were to do, but it seems that Aborigines in their traditional societies usually needed less than forty hours a week to sustain their material requirements.) Although white settlers later thought that Aboriginal camp life was casual, it operated according to the strict rules that governed Aboriginal affairs. Some of these rules dealt with food distribution, in which the basic principle was sharing.

Blackened oven stones and fire stones still mark a number of the former campsites, where large animals such as kangaroos, wallabies and emus were often baked in ovens hollowed out of the ground. Hot stones could be placed in the ovens to provide heat; hot coals and ashes were used to cook smaller animals, fish, lizards and birds. A thick coating of mud might be smeared around a large bird, such as a black swan, before cooking. Cooking methods varied throughout the continent, but baking and roasting were always popular. Boiling and stewing, however, were not practised, as there were no suitable containers.

In temporary camps Aborigines normally made do with shelters of a lighter kind or just simple windbreaks. In desert areas separate shelters could be erected for shade during the day. A specialist hut-builder could do the

A seashore encampment, Rapid Bay, South Australia, in the 1840s

Flying foxes being placed in an earth oven and then covered with sand, central Arnhem Land

work. Substantial huts were erected in the more frequented camps. Some camps resembled small villages of an almost permanent kind. In fertile areas many Aborigines were living in these camps, in virtually non-nomadic fashion, when Europeans arrived in 1788. Coastal huts in the Botany Bay district and in Tasmania indicated this. Captain Sturt also found a group of about seventy huts on the bank of the Macquarie River in New South Wales, and J.T. Gellibrand reported a group of about a hundred while on a trip to Port Phillip in 1836. These campsites could feature the large material articles such as canoes and rafts used by groups along the coasts or rivers, or animal and fish nets, often reaching about a hundred metres in length. But personal possessions were not conspicuous: traditional Aboriginal society needed no store of personal goods for daily living. In fact such goods would have proved burdens to a people who wanted

freedom of movement. Even essential items like grinding stones were often too heavy to carry and had to be left at different camps.

Cooking a kangaroo in an earth oven

Weapons and other Material Items

Weapons could be noticed in many Aboriginal camps. Spears were usually the most prominent. These were used chiefly for hunting, but occasionally, too, for fighting, ceremonial purposes and play. Varying in type and length—the longest being about four metres—spears were tipped with bone, hardwood, stone or even an echidna spine. Some spears had several barbs, capable of anchoring the spear in its target. The reed spear, made by inserting a shaped and pointed piece of hardwood into a shaft of stout reed, was common along the River Murray. (To fasten the hardwood end of the reed spear, Aborigines tied it with sinews from a kangaroo and then applied gum.) Spears, however, as in Tasmania, were often simply long, slender sticks, straightened by heating and being pointed at the end—and still very effective.

To provide more leverage, many spears were thrown with a spear-thrower or throwing-stick (*woomera*, or *wommera*), which had a peg attached to fit into the notched end of the spear. A stone chisel could be fastened to the handle end. The spear-thrower had several other uses, for example as a handy bowl or digging implement. The

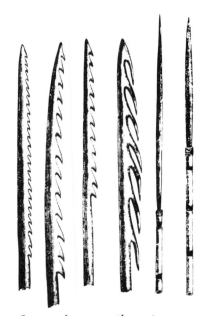

Spears from south-eastern Australia: the four on the left were used for fighting; the two on the right are reed spears, with a hardwood end fastened into a reed

A spear held in a spear-thrower, ready for throwing. Note the short peg, cut from the stick itself or tied to it and fitting into the hollow end of the spear

spear-thrower was not known in Tasmania (nor were barbed spears), but in its various designs—broad and bowl-shaped, or narrow—it gave greater speed and accuracy to the spear. One early European observer noted:

It enables a man to throw a spear with much force and great accuracy. Its simplicity and its perfect adaptation to the uses for which it is designed, strengthen one's belief in the natural genius of this people.[12]

The Aboriginal spear-thrower has become well known. So has the boomerang, especially the returning boomerang. Boomerangs were known among other peoples, in America, India and Egypt, but the Australian Aborigines invented the returning type and were its only users. Boomerangs were patiently carved from curved hardwood, which was heated and bent to give the returning boomerang its distinctive lengthwise twist. A returning boomerang was mostly for play, though it could be thrown to scare birds into a net strung across a river and then itself return to land.

Non-returning, or killing, boomerangs were often larger and not so curved. These were dangerous weapons, capable of inflicting serious injury during fights. They were used for hunting, too, and for cutting meat, for stirring the fire when cooking, and for clearing the site for a camp. Non-returning boomerangs were unknown in Tasmania and parts of northern Australia, while returning boomerangs had an even more restricted range.

Another weapon was the club, or waddy, often known as a *nulla nulla*. Like the boomerang, it had a variety of shapes and decorations and was employed for hunting as well as fighting. To ward off such weapons, the best defence was to use a shield or the base of the broad throwing-stick. Aborigines in Central Australia also used

Wooden clubs once used in Victoria

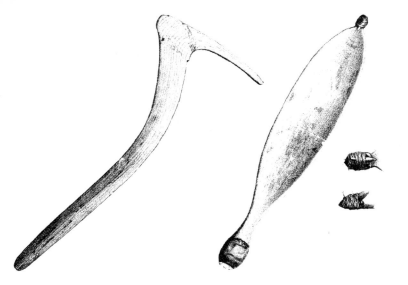

the shield to defend themselves in fights in which stone knives were used.

Stone, wood and bone were serviceable materials for making implements. Stone implements enabled many tasks to be performed. Grinding stones crushed fruits of the inland *nardoo* plant and grass seeds into a paste; stone pounders beat mallee bark into fibrous mats; stone hatchets gouged footholds in trees or cut bark sheets for a canoe. To carve sacred objects, to fashion spears, to cut meat, in fact to accomplish a host of cutting, carving and scraping operations, the Aborigines used other stone implements, often finely shaped and of quite small size. The patience and skill required to make such objects is explained in the description of an Aranda man making a hatchet:

First, a large, rounded, diorite pebble is taken; then with a lump of quartz the workman removes fairly large chips, bringing the stone down to something like the proposed

A fighting boomerang, a spear-thrower and its pegs, and a shield (rear and front view), from the Horn Expedition to Central Australia in the 1890s

Grinding stones formerly used along the Darling River to grind grass seeds

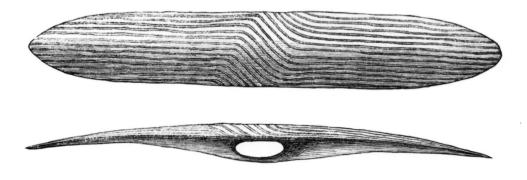

dimensions. This done, a rounded pebble of quartzite is brought into requisition, and for a day or even two, he will sit, probably upon his heels, and patiently tap away, hour after hour, at the surface, taking off small flakes, until no sign of the original rough working is left. Then one of the nardoo mills, blocks of stone which are brought long distances, sometimes on the backs of women, for grinding seeds, is brought into use as a grindstone. With sand and water the axe is rubbed down until the surfaces are smooth; next comes the hafting; a withy is made and bent round the blunt portion of the stone till it holds it tightly; then the two halves of the withy are joined half-way down with two pieces of grass or other string. The next operation is to squeeze a lump of softened porcupine grass resin in between the haft and the stone; this done, a fire-stick smooths down the resin, and nothing more remains than to decorate the haft with red ochre.[13]

A hatchet, as used by Aborigines who lived near Melbourne. The wooden handle was 38 cm long; the stone head, 13 cm long and 5 cm wide

(*diorite*—a variety of stone; *hafting*—the fixing of the handle; *withy*—a light, flexible wooden tie)

Stone tools survive from some of the oldest Aboriginal sites in Australia. Aborigines were possibly the first people in the world to use certain techniques for grinding stone. A study of stone tools of different ages, especially of methods of flaking and sharpening, shows that techniques of working stone changed over the centuries— revealing again that Aboriginal society was not static. Stone tools were originally core tools of the 'horsehoof' type—lumpy, hand-held choppers with a flaked cutting edge—together with flakes for cutting and scraping.

A nineteenth century Western Australian shield, about 84 cm long and 15 cm wide, used in a half-kneeling or stooping position in combat

A stone fighting pick from Barrow Creek, Northern Territory

These tools were used in crafting wooden tools, as well as being useful for other tasks. Later, especially in the last 5 000 years, smaller stone tools such as spear points, adze flakes and blades became common. Some of the finest stone tools were the hatchet heads, with their carefully ground edges; these were used in hatchets (wielded in one hand) as early as 20 000 years ago in northern Australia and from more recent times in southern Australia.

Like stone, wood was very important and frequently used for different purposes. Log rafts, weapons, domestic utensils, sacred objects and message-sticks were some of the wooden products. The wooden digging-stick was one of the best-known items in Aboriginal daily life—at least to women. This implement, sharpened at one or both ends and usually fire-hardened, was invaluable in the women's skilful daily foraging. Its use in finding yams gave it the name of a yam-stick, though women also wielded it for fighting. Many other items came from bark: buckets in the Kimberleys, canoes, huts, sleeping-mats,

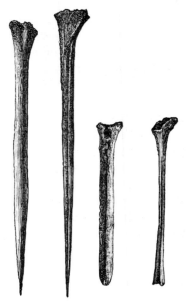

Bone awls for piercing holes when making rugs, and bone spatulas for smoothing seams

Pearl-shell fish-hooks from Queensland, showing various stages in making them

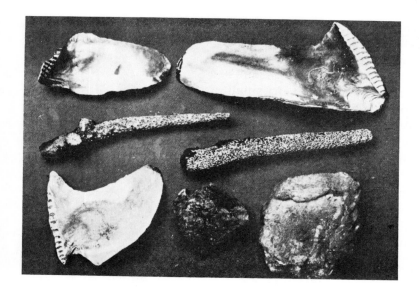

Queensland shell knives, coral files and quartz implements

clothing, sandals, and wrapping material for carrying food or keeping a baby warm. Shell, bone, gum, grass, palm-leaves, animal skins and human hair were among other useful materials. The shell of an emu egg, for example, made a handy cup. Animal bone and tortoise-shell were ideal for awls or fish-hooks. Resin, or gum, obtained from spinifex and several varieties of trees, was the Aboriginal plastic, important as a cement. Kangaroo-grass was suitable for making nets, while water containers could be made from possum skins or palm leaves. The Aborigines were thus skilled in using all the resources of the environment to meet their needs.

Trade

The trading (exchanging) of goods and ideas was a feature of Aboriginal life. Traders followed pathways—some being the pathways along which spirit-ancestors were supposed to have travelled—across the continent. Items of value found their way to distant groups and helped to keep traditional Aboriginal life vital. Through trade, local groups could get raw materials unobtainable in their local territory, together with articles made by skilled craftsmen elsewhere. Materials highly desired, such as ochre, *pituri* and skin rugs, were thus spread far and wide. Shell from northern Australia was traded far into the south of the continent. Sometimes trading was centred at a special place such as Kopperamanna on Cooper Creek in north-eastern South Australia—here soft-wood shields, spear cane, boomerangs, hatchet-heads from Queensland and the south, and prized red ochre from a quarry near Beltana in the Flinders Ranges were among the items exchanged. Groups of Aborigines also opened up small quarries of stone for special purposes. Victorian greenstone—especially from the Mount William quarry in Central Victoria, which was supervised by a special custodian—was coveted for axe-heads. (Billi-Billeri, Mount William's last custodian, died in 1846.) Stone from this and other quarries, such as the Moore Creek quarry in the New England district of New South Wales, was widely traded. Skilled craftsmen in Aboriginal societies found a ready demand for their manufactures: the Warramunga and Tjingilli peoples, for example, made knives eagerly sought among their Central Australian neighbours.

Traders had no special form of currency, and the trade in ideas, art forms and rituals also spread over vast areas. The Indonesian and Papuan influences were carried into the interior. Other ceremonial practices, language and social customs were transported between Aborigines when trade in material items took place. (Today surviving rock engravings show representations of objects or fauna remote from their original localities.) Aboriginal traders would occasionally travel hundreds of kilometres on their journeys, carrying message-sticks or decorated spears to enable them to pass easily through other groups' lands. But such travel, often occupying about ten days, could also be dangerous, and trading parties had to be ready to fight. The return of traders to a camp was often the cause for great celebrations.

A wooden-hafted stone knife, made by the Warramunga people in the early twentieth century

Camp Life

A powerful element in Aboriginal daily life was fire. By day it could be used for cooking; during the night small fires could be kindled alongside sleeping-places. Yet fire was not just a source of heat. As well as its use in 'firestick farming', fire could be employed for driving out game, for sending signals, and for light at night. (A tiny fire on a canoe could even be lit to attract fish at night for spearing.) The smoke from a fire at the front of a hut served to ward off mosquitoes. Fire also played an important role in ceremonies such as initiation ordeals. Fire had even further importance:

The [Aborigine] looks upon fire as one of the great indispensable quantities of his social existence; it is the element which dispels the evil spirits from his camp; it is the means by which comfort and friendship are made accessible to him; it is his universal companion. More than this, it is the fire, with its warmth and its light, which draws individuals, families, groups, and tribes together and through its agency and influence that social concourse is established which lies at the bottom of all conviviality, oracular discussion, and ceremony.[14]

The Aborigines had a number of explanations for the origins of fire. The Warramunga people believed two hawk ancestors first made fire by rubbing two sticks together. This story was passed down through the generations, and mentioned a common method by which Aborigines made fire. The method took skill: it involved rubbing a hardwood stick or boomerang vigorously across a piece of softwood to produce smouldering wood powder. The powder, placed on dry grass, leaves or bark, was then blown until a flame resulted.

Another method, more widely adopted, followed the same principle. An Aborigine used a stick as a drill, twirling its point rapidly into a shield or into another stick

Two photographs showing fire making by sawing hardwood across a softer piece of wood and then dropping dry grass on to the heated wood

held firmly underfoot. Again smouldering wood powder was produced to ignite other material. A third method, practised at times in South Australia and western New South Wales, was to strike a piece of flint against ironstone. The resulting sparks started dry tinder burning.

Aboriginal men were responsible for making fire and for carrying the fire-making sticks when the camp was moved. But making fire required patience and effort, so glowing fire-sticks were frequently taken from one campsite to another. This was often the job of the women, whose duties included gathering firewood as well as carrying children, domestic articles and water. Men travelled more lightly burdened, prepared for hunting as they moved along.

On the Australian mainland, dogs were as much a part of camp life as fire. Before 1788 these dogs were dingoes that had been tamed, usually from the puppy stage; dingoes also remained in the wild. When white people arrived in Australia new breeds of dogs were introduced, often interbreeding with those of the Aborigines. There was a great bond of affection between Aborigines and

Fire making by the drilling method, as depicted in 1847

Striking stone flakes to make stone tools—a Wailbri man, Northern Territory

their dogs: dogs were treated as family members and allowed to share the warmth of fires and beds. They were not trained to hunt, but remained about the camp, eating scraps of food and giving companionship to the people. The dogs also contributed to the noise of the camp, adding their yelping to the gossip of the people and the laughter of the children at play.

Aboriginal camps could be scenes of much activity. Women spent time there caring for children, preparing food, weaving baskets and mats, and carrying out other tasks. Men could be busy making or repairing weapons and implements, cutting their hair, or simply recovering energy after vigorous hunting. Ceremonial occasions were also planned in the camps, with ornamentation

Wailbri men making stone hatchets

being prepared for them. But whatever activity was undertaken, the special rules applying throughout Aboriginal society were maintained. Not only was the camp
itself carefully sited in relation to water and weather, but
the position of each hut and the sleeping-place of each
person were fixed according to customary laws, so that
married people and single individuals, children and
visitors, all had their own places in the camp.

The Pattern of Aboriginal Life

Traditional Aboriginal society was quite different from
many other societies. The idea of working a certain number of hours each day and building up a store of
possessions or money was absent. Aborigines were
nevertheless skilled in satisfying their needs. It was an
advantage, too, for a hunter-gatherer people to have only
essential physical items to carry.

To survive in the demanding Australian environment
Aborigines needed a vast knowledge and understanding
of the land. With this knowledge and understanding they
fared quite well in conditions which later overcame many
Europeans. Although they did not build great reservoirs,
cultivate the soil, or rear animals, Aborigines had an un-
rivalled ability to find food and water. They could read
the signs of the bush to perfection—every track was
recognised, every seasonal change meant new things to
hunt, every watering-place on their land was known.

From 1788 European settlers in Australia described
Aboriginal society as 'primitive' and 'stone age'. This
judgment was made by people who not only believed
in the natural superiority of European civilisation but
were anxious to justify their seizure of the land. Among
other things Europeans pointed out the Aboriginal lack
of metals and machines. They tended to ignore the fact
that Aborigines had managed their environment effectively and could skilfully perform a multitude of tasks.
This ability to manage the environment had not been acquired easily, and years of instruction were necessary for
each new generation to learn the arts of living in this
environment.

Europeans also usually regarded Aboriginal society as
much the same across the whole continent. This opinion
was formed too hastily. It ignored the variations in
material culture, languages and ritual between different

*A nineteenth century
illustration of Aboriginal
men fishing from a bark
canoe. A small fire,
burning on wet weeds and
sand between the two men,
attracted the fish. The
method was often used on
the Murray and Darling
rivers*

groups. Other hasty European judgments were that Aboriginal society was static and unchanging, and that Aborigines did not alter their environment. Yet evidence from the past shows that Aborigines refined their technical skills during centuries of living in Australia. They did not have a static society, nor did they passively accept the conditions around them—the building of dams for catching eels, the practice of firestick farming, and the speedy adoption of Indonesian and Papuan customs were examples of that.

Europeans made a further judgment about Aborigines and their culture. Noticing that Aborigines could often be seen resting and sleeping in their camps, European settlers accused them of laziness. This charge came from misunderstanding the nature of Aboriginal society. Apart from attending to their various daily tasks in camps, Aborigines usually preferred not to follow the European pattern of work, with its emphasis on gaining material goods and profit. Instead, with its rich ceremonial life

A bark canoe being constructed on the River Murray in 1862. The bark sheet, propped up at the edges and with stones and logs to weigh it in the middle, was heated by fire underneath and inside. The heated sap made the canoe soft and pliable until it dried to the shape required

and its carefully framed rules, the Aborigines' daily pattern of living emphasised a different relationship with the land, one which did not involve 'profit', 'work', 'laziness' or other European ideas. This relationship, and other aspects of Aboriginal social life, are discussed in the next chapter.

1 Harney, W.E. *North of 23°*, Australasian Publishing Co., Sydney, n.d., p. 67.
2 Mountford, C. *Brown Men and Red Sand*, Robertson and Mullens, Melbourne, 1948, p. 59.
3 White, S.A. *In the Far North-West*, W.K. Thomas and Co., Adelaide, 1916, p. 82.
4 Harney, W.E. op. cit. p. 69.
5 McCarthy, F.D. *Australia's Aborigines—Their Life and Culture*, Colorgravure Publications, Melbourne, 1957, p. 60.
6 Banfield, E.J. *Confessions of a Beachcomber*, T. Fisher Unwin, London, 1910, p. 245.
7 Legge, R.W. 'Tasmanian Aboriginal Middens of the West Coast', in *Report of the Nineteenth Meeting of the Australasian Association for the Advancement of Science*, Hobart, 1929, p. 327.
8 Bride, T.F. *Letters from Victorian Pioneers* . . . Public Library, Melbourne, 1898, p. 219.
9 Smyth, R. Brough *The Aborigines of Victoria* . . . Government Printer, Melbourne, 1878, vol. 2, p. 248.
10 Abbie, A.A. *The Original Australians*, A.H. and A.W. Reed, Wellington, 1969, p. 83.
11 Spencer, Baldwin *Wanderings in Wild Australia*, Macmillan and Co., London, 1928, vol. 1, pp. 158–59.
12 Smyth, R. Brough op. cit. vol. 1, p. 310.
13 Thomas, N.W. *Natives of Australia*, Constable and Co., London, 1906, pp. 48–49.
14 Basedow, H. *The Australian Aboriginal*, F.W. Preece and Sons, Adelaide, 1925, pp. 258–59.

ABORIGINAL SOCIETY

3

The previous chapter described ways in which Aborigines satisfied their physical needs in their traditional societies, developing a material culture to enable them to live in often inhospitable parts of Australia. They came to terms with their environment, learning how to obtain food, how to craft implements and how to perform other daily tasks. It may seem that their obvious skill in providing for material needs was the main reason for the continuing existence and survival of Aborigines in Australia for more than thirty thousand years.

Yet Aborigines did not rely solely on their ability to perform material tasks. A powerful reason for the strength and persistence of the Aboriginal occupation of Australia was the carefully regulated social life of the people. Aboriginal society was not loose or without structure, and thus did not resemble the usual picture that whites gave of it. Nor was it unrefined or barbaric, nor lawless. Aborigines were very careful about their personal relationships. Each person had a clearly defined place in Aboriginal society. Rules were carefully drawn up and observed, so that arrangements about matters such as marriage, religious duties and contact with other people were all part of a strict pattern of behaviour binding social groups together. Courtesy, too, was a feature of much of their conduct.

This chapter looks at the social life of the Aboriginal people. Once again it describes their traditional society in the past tense, examining social life at its fullest stage before the white invasion of Australia altered it so much. It should be remembered, however, that Aborigines today observe many of the traditional social customs, obligations and relationships.

Birth and Childhood

Aborigines have always been noted for giving fond attention to their children. In traditional society this was done from birth to the time of initiation into the secrets of adulthood. A child's birth, as with other events in the Aboriginal world, was believed to be not solely a human affair. It was commonly believed that a spirit-child, from somewhere in the landscape, entered a woman's body at the time of conception. This belief carried with it the idea of reincarnation—the spirit-ancestors had left spirit-children behind them, who were then born again through humans. In turn the spirit of a dead person would go back to an old camping-place, often to a certain tree or waterhole, and wait until it chose a woman for birth again, perhaps changing its sex at each reincarnation.

Often a pregnant woman, and sometimes her husband too, had to observe certain restrictions, especially about eating particular foods. It was common for a woman about to give birth to remove herself from a camp. A companion might help her, though childbirth usually occurred without difficulty. In many areas a woman would have to resume her normal life as quickly as possible, perhaps even on the day of the birth having a long walk to rejoin her local group. A baby would be cradled and carried in a sheet of bark or animal skin, or carried in a *coolamon* which was sometimes placed on the mother's head. The baby was not clothed, but a mother's body would give warmth at night. When older, a baby was often carried on its mother's back. Babies were breast-fed for a considerable time, and brought up in close daily contact with adults and other children.

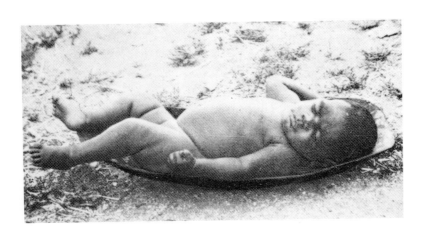

An Aranda baby asleep in a pitchi, *early twentieth century*

From early days young children became familiar with the company of others and life in a group. Yet they retained a strong bond to their parents, who took special care of them. Parents taught children their first words, though there was care about the names given to children. At first, children were known simply by a term such as 'child' or 'little brother', depending on the relationship. Older relatives would decide a child's name to be given at initiation, but this adult name, regarded as having

A young Aboriginal child eating a wood grub, Musgrave Ranges, South Australia

sacred significance, would often be kept quite secret—
'our fathers have told us that we must never speak of our
secret names', said a Kurnai man from Gippsland, describing the common practice in his area.[1] This sacred
aspect of the use of names usually led to a dead person's
name not being mentioned. In life a person's nickname
was commonly employed, or the person might simply be
known by the name of the clan or group.

In the family group a child also had a special relationship to a certain person. Often, with a boy, this was to
his mother's brother or brothers. This person, the child's
uncle, would act as a guardian and be responsible for
educating him in the secret life of his people at initiation
and other times. The same person might select a husband
for a girl child, his niece. These relationships were of extreme importance and at the heart of the Aboriginal social
system.

Young children enjoyed considerable freedom. Their
parents frequently played with them and taught them
dances and songs. Some activities were good training for
adult life: boys took part in sham fights, throwing toy
spears or balls of mud, while girls had mock duels with
sticks. Games such as handball, hide-and-seek, mud slid-
ing and skipping were popular, as were water games and
swimming. Children also played make-believe games and
fashioned clever string figures from a length of vine cord
or string made from plants. Mimicking the activities of
adults was another favourite pastime.

Older children undertook many practical activities.
These gave children training for adult life, imparting
skills through experience rather than theory. Girls
learned about gathering food and preparing meals by as-
sisting their mothers. Boys were directed more towards
the hunting carried out by males, beginning to recognise
the calls and notes of animals and birds. They came to
recognise the tracks of game, until they could even dis-
tinguish between individuals of the same species. They
began to hunt for reptiles and birds and gather food for
the camp.

Parents gradually demanded more from their children,
requiring them to understand their responsibilities as
members of a group. Proper behaviour towards parents
was expected. Then as children grew older they learned
songs and dances, preparing for the important future
learning of ceremonial songs and dances. They also
learned to bear pain and hunger, which they would

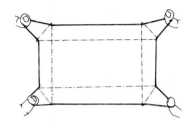

*Diagrams showing steps in
making a string-figure
design of a dugong*

probably experience in ceremonies and on other occasions in later life.

Initiation

The end of childhood was an important stage, in which
the respected adult members of an Aboriginal group
played a major role. For boys it was the occasion for
ceremonies, instruction and ordeals, forming the period
of initiation. In general, traditional Aboriginal society emphasised the importance of males, and boys' initiation
was regarded as very significant. Yet girls, too, often had
to undergo a similar, though less intense, process. Girls'
initiation activities began as puberty was reached; these
sometimes involved some physical marking, considered a
test as well as a sign of more adult status. At the end of
her training a girl left her parents' camp and, with little
fuss, was married, usually to someone quite a few years
older. But her performance of rituals remained important
to her: women had their own ceremonies and sacred ob-
servances in their adult years.

For boys, initiation was a landmark in their lives,
although its timing and manner could vary in different
groups. It usually began at the age of puberty, between
twelve and sixteen, when boys were separated from most
of their close relatives and normal camp life. It could continue for a very long time, beginning with various tests
and ordeals and extending through several other
ceremonies. Sacred objects could be revealed to the in-
itiates; secret rituals could be experienced and learned. It
might be years rather than months before the person
could return to more normal camp life. When he did so,
it was as a man, not a boy. He was now ready to share
in the sacred life of the people.

In physical terms the testing and ordeals were intended
to strengthen a person's physical and mental qualities as
a preparation for adult responsibilities. The physical part
of initiation was merely the outward sign of the vital
process—the recognition of a person's maturity and the
passing on of some of the sacred ritual and secrets of the
group. Initiation meant the end of childhood; it also
meant the beginning of the full ceremonial and religious
life which adults observed. Initiated people began to play
an increasing role in rituals and ceremony, learning more
and more about the secret life. They gained great respect

for the elders, those who were the guardians of the wis-
dom passed down from generation to generation.

Marriage and Womanhood

At birth, or perhaps before, a girl often had a husband
chosen for her, according to strict rules, by a close male
relative or relatives. The families involved carefully
respected this arrangement. As the girl grew up, the
families saw that certain duties were carried out and exchanged gifts. Often the marriage arrangements included
the exchange of other sisters and nieces between the
groups. A girl began to live in her husband's camp at the
age of puberty. Since her husband could have more than
one wife—often Aboriginal males had several—the girl
might have to share the camp with an older wife. To the
Aborigines, a practical people, a new wife was valued for
the help she could give in food gathering and in carrying
family belongings. Her life did not seem easy, and she
might even suffer occasional physical punishment from
her husband, though she was capable of defending herself by well-chosen words or actually fighting back. She
had to be courageous, enduring difficulties and physical
pain with little complaint. Yet an Aboriginal woman's life
was not always harsh, nor was she a person whose
nature became hardened by it. It has been said of her:

An Aranda woman and child, early twentieth century

Generally speaking she can be as kind and generous as any
other woman: loving and fiercely defensive of her children,
charitably tolerant of her husband and readily aroused to
sympathy by the misfortune of others, especially children. The
women love to chatter, gossip and joke among themselves,
banter with the men and watch their children play. They enjoy
adorning themselves . . . Above all they endure a harsh
existence stoically . . .[2]

When Europeans arrived in Australia they were quick
to criticise the apparent lack of affection in traditional
Aboriginal society between some husbands and their
wives. They also attacked the wife-lending, polygamy
and jealousy that occurred from time to time. Yet
Aborigines, as mentioned before, were careful about their
personal relationships. Their society consisted of a number of different social groups in which the position of
each person was carefully established. Non-Aborigines

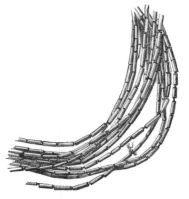

Part of a reed necklace (478 pieces in all, strung on twine), once owned by a woman of the Burdekin area, Queensland

Contents of an Aboriginal woman's bag, suggesting some activities of daily life. (From George Grey, Journals of Two Expeditions of Discovery, *T. and W. Boone, London, 1841, vol. 2, pp. 266–67)*

The contents of a native woman's bag are:—A flat stone to pound roots with; earth to mix with the pounded roots; quartz, for the purpose of making spears and knives; stones for hatchets; prepared cakes of gum, to make and mend weapons, and implements; kangaroo sinews to make spears and to sew with; needles made of the shin bones of kangaroos, with which they sew their cloaks, bags, &c.; opossum hair to be spun into waist belts; shavings of kangaroo skins to polish spears, &c.; the shell of a species of mussel to cut hair, &c. with; native knives; a native hatchet; pipe clay; red ochre, or burnt clay; yellow ochre; a piece of paper bark to carry water in; waistbands, and spare ornaments; pieces of quartz, which the native doctors have extracted from their patients, and thus cured them from diseases; these they preserve as carefully as Europeans do relics. Banksia cones (small ones), or pieces of a dry white species of fungus, to kindle fire with rapidity, and to convey it from place to place; grease, if they can procure it from a whale, or from any other source; the spare weapons of their husbands, or the pieces of wood from which these are to be manufactured; the roots, &c. which they have collected during the day. Skins not yet prepared for cloaks are generally carried between the bag and the back, so as to form a sort of cushion for the bag to rest on.

have usually misunderstood this system; those who have tried to understand it in detail have noted how complicated the system can be, but how carefully and how well it controls social life.

Language ('Tribal') Groups

After 1788 the European term most commonly used in
referring to units of traditional Aboriginal society was the
word 'tribe'. White settlers also referred to 'chiefs' leading the tribes. At the time, such terms were commonly
used about American Indians, Africans and other
peoples. But Aborigines had no 'chiefs' in the usual
sense, nor did Aborigines themselves strongly identify
with a larger group of people like a tribe. Nor did they
actually feel themselves to be members of a race called
Aborigines, another term used by whites. (Because 'Aborigines' has been imposed on them, the people today
often reject that name.) In the case of the the term 'tribe',
while it has proved convenient to use it for large, somewhat distinct groups of people, a 'tribe' was not the most
vital group in traditional society to which Aborigines felt
they belonged. All the members of a language group or
'tribe', for example, seldom or never met together. There
was no central governing body that organised the affairs
of such a group, nor did the group work as a single
economic body. Clans and the small local groups were of
much greater importance in Aboriginal society.

What, then, was the larger, 'tribal' group? It was a collection of people, numbering from about a hundred to as
many as fifteen hundred, speaking a common language
and sharing similar customs and beliefs. There were
probably several hundred such groups inhabiting the
continent in 1788. Each unit should thus be called a language group rather than a tribe; its members also usually
acknowledged a distinct name for the group. It occupied
a recognised area of land, and all members living within
that area believed themselves to be related. Sometimes
the differences between the language groups were
blurred: the dialects or languages of neighbouring groups
could be quite similar, allowing easy communication between them, and common boundaries might not be
firmly fixed. Sometimes a common name was applied to
several groups or sub-groups (such as the Ngarrindjeri
along the lower Murray in South Australia). Normally,
however, different language groups had no strong bonds.
The language group was a loose-knit body, which in
more extreme cases, such as the Aranda in Central
Australia, appeared to be in process of breaking up into
separate groups.

While each language group had its own territory, this

territory was not regarded merely as a place for obtaining food and performing other daily tasks. It was the Aborigines' spirit-home, in which ancestral spirits had lived and still lived. Thus Aborigines were bound to their land by strong Dreaming ties, which made them very reluctant to leave it. When Aborigines referred to 'their country' they meant not just the area where they gathered food but the home of their ancestral spirits. Within that land were many sacred sites, which gave the land far more than economic importance. In fact it has been said that the land really owned the Aborigines, rather than the reverse.

The Local Group, the Family, and Kinship

As mentioned, the language group or 'tribe' was a less important unit than the local group. The local group has often been known as a horde or band. (Unfortunately terms such as horde, band and clan have been used in various ways by different observers—a sign of the difficulty of understanding the complex social life of the Aboriginal people.) The local group was composed of closely related families who lived together from day to day, hunting and food-gathering over their own area of land, to which they also had close spiritual ties. This was the group in which Aborigines spent much of their daily time, and to which they were very loyal. Members worked together for the common good. Food was shared according to strict rules, so that the old as well as the

A diagram showing how an Aboriginal boy, in a family of three children, would classify some of his near relatives. Note that under this system he would have another father, mother, brother and sister instead of another uncle, aunt and cousins

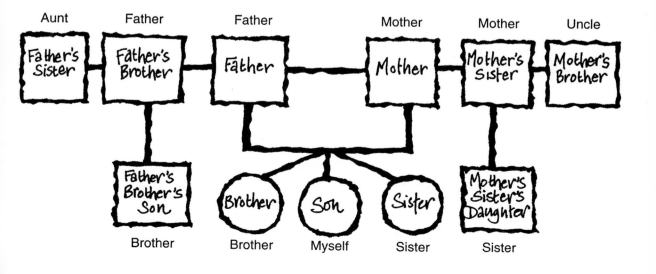

young were provided for. The families within such a local
group often acted by themselves, and were the basic
units of the group; they were related to other families in
the group usually through the father, so that the group
was formed around close male relatives of different
generations. Sons born to members of the group would
stay in it all their lives, but normally could not marry a
girl within it. Daughters would leave the group when
joining their husbands, but remain members of the clan
which had spirit-homes in the old locality.

In Aboriginal society the basic family unit—a man, his
wife or wives, and their children—was always very important. Strong bonds existed between its members and
members of the local group. In fact the bonds went further, since Aboriginal people regarded themselves as
linked in groups of relatives. Behind this idea were the
beliefs of kinship, which varied in some places and can
be very difficult to understand. Basically, kinship rules
considered some of the relatives of the same generation
as equal, so that to an Aboriginal male his father's
brothers were all regarded as 'fathers', not uncles, while
their male children were regarded as 'brothers', not
cousins. On his mother's side, her sisters were regarded
as 'mothers', and their daughters as 'sisters'. (On the
other hand, father's sisters and mother's brothers were
regarded as 'aunts' and 'uncles'.) Aborigines thus
grouped a number of relatives under a similar name. Kinship groups existed, and each 'skin group', as it was
sometimes known, had its own name and customs. Marriages were arranged to members of other kinship
groups, often between people recognised as cousins.
Great care was taken to see that incest was avoided. Thus
Aborigines grew up learning carefully about relationships. Their ideas about how relatives were classified,
and about the proper manner of conduct towards them,
formed strict rules governing personal behaviour.

These ideas of kinship and of groupings such as
moieties, sections and subsections within Aboriginal
society remain complicated. Moieties, for example, were
two other divisions into which people were often classified, according to their fathers' or mothers' bloodlines;
this system helped to guard against marriages between
close relatives. Sections (there were four sections in many
language groups) were further divisions. Though little
detail about these groups can be given here, the important point is that social relationships and patterns of

An Aboriginal drawing in the 19th century, showing Aborigines in duels

behaviour towards other people were strongly influenced by the kinship system, which dealt with many matters besides the allowable choice of a marriage partner. Under this system Aborigines avoided possible conflict with certain people, such as mothers-in-law, by limiting contact between them (they were not to speak to each other). The same system required the performance of religious and other duties, and guided arrangements about the proper sharing of food. In this well-ordered society rules had to be respected, for the welfare of all. If rules were broken, punishment followed, either by verbal admonishing or by physical means, and in extreme cases even death. Disagreements were often settled by duelling with spears, clubs or digging-sticks until first blood was drawn. Usually disputes were settled as soon as possible, so that the peaceful pattern of group life could be restored. Occasionally, however, some hostile attitudes between different parties lingered for years, overflowing into violent clashes, injuries and deaths. But wide-scale fighting—'tribal wars', as Europeans imagined it—was not part of traditional Aboriginal society.

Law and the Elders

Early European settlers in Australia generally thought that Aborigines lived in a lawless state. Yet respect for Aboriginal laws was required—and enforced—among Aborigines in traditional society. The ancestral spirits, above all, had laid down expected patterns of behaviour. Neglect of these sacred obligations was an offence, from which punishments resulted. There were also offences against people and property. It is important to note, however, that laws and patterns of expected behaviour were not established by Aboriginal 'governments', of the

European kind. There was no single, central government, nor were there law courts to decide disputes and punishments.

Perhaps the nearest thing to a ruling body in traditional society was the group of elders, usually men. Great respect was shown for these recognised elders, whose grey hair usually marked them out from others. Yet it was not merely old age that distinguished them, for some were younger, active men whose abilities and wise counsel were acknowledged. The elders were known for their experience in practical affairs and for their knowledge of sacred matters. From time to time they could act as an informal council and make decisions affecting group members. They could settle arguments and decide courses of action to be followed. Perhaps one elder would be particularly important and his advice would thus be specially heeded, though he was not a king or chief. In fact the elders were not simply judges or lawmakers but rather teachers of their fellow people.

The Spiritual Life

Behind all social arrangements—indeed behind all Aboriginal life—was a powerful set of religious beliefs. Aboriginal life can not be understood without reference to them. Again this can be seen in the Aboriginal relationship to the land. Individuals did not own land in the European sense—the land they occupied was passed down from previous generations and entrusted to them. As has been mentioned, the land seemed to own *them*, not the opposite, since the land was the spiritual home of their ancestors, who included the ancestral beings who had wandered the land in the creation time. Thus Aborigines regarded this land, and the parts of it occupied by local groups, as entrusted to their care, rather than owned for practical purposes. The clans were important in land-owning matters. Clans were groups of people related by descent from a common ancestor, sometimes human, sometimes non-human. These groups would jealously guard their spirit-homes, including the sacred sites of their clan and their sacred rituals, totems and songs.

The Aborigine was a very religious person whose life was strongly shaped by spiritual beliefs. The anthropologist F.D. McCarthy explained the importance of religion in traditional Aboriginal society:

To the initiated man his religion explains the origin of life itself and of his tribal customs, the source of his supply of food and raw materials, and the mysterious world beyond the comprehension of his scientific or general knowledge. To him it is a religion of great sanctity, inspiring in its mythology and songs, and impressive in its often colourful ceremonies . . . It becomes a most important part of the adult life of the men, demanding a great deal of time and energy in the enactment of ritual, a tremendous concentration of intelligence in the memorisation of the myths, song-cycles, ritual procedure and art designs, and an absolute faith in the efficacy of the beliefs and ceremonial activities.[3]

At the heart of Aboriginal religion was the idea of the Dreaming, outlined in Chapter One. This idea was kept alive in the stories about the spirit-ancestors, stories varying among Aboriginal groups but usually rich in detail. These are often referred to as myths, though to Aborigines they were not myths but truths forming the basis of social life. The spirit-ancestors, as outlined above,

A stone arrangement on a ceremonial ground at Woomera, South Australia. The extensive stone arrangement was made by clearing gibbers and making an irregular outline with stones

laid down patterns of behaviour that had to be followed—failure to observe these and carry out the proper
rituals could lead to a lack of rain or food, as well as
punishment for the wrongdoer.

Again it was customary for the fully initiated men, and
especially the elders, to be the guardians of these traditional cults and responsible for passing them on to the
next generation. These men had the greatest knowledge
of the traditions and determined when the appropriate
rituals were to be held. The rituals were dramatic perfor-
mances in which acting, singing and dancing were very
important. The parts had to be learned by heart, and the
whole performance had greater significance because the
actors seemed to become the ancestral beings themselves.
The ceremonies were held on sacred ground and usually
could not be seen by the unitiated or members of the
female sex. As part of the rituals, designs of great totemic
significance were painted on the bodies of the participants, on the ground, on rock surfaces or on sacred
objects. For this purpose the Aborigines used ochre,
human blood and birds' down. A headdress of grass,
twigs and human hair could complete the decoration.

The whole effect of the material decoration was very
colourful. Other objects, too, gave vital meaning to the
sacred ceremonies. These were the visual representations
of the sacred life. Natural features such as trees, hills and
groups of boulders frequently had sacred significance,
but smaller portable objects of wood or stone also had
special meaning. They were part of the separate sacred
life of both men and women, and were kept secret by
each sex.

The Natural World and Totemism

The Aboriginal people clearly lived very close to nature,
or more correctly, regarded themselves as at one with nature—part of a natural order in which animals, plants and
Aborigines were linked together. The heavens, too, were
part of this natural order. The sky seemed always close,
in fact only a little higher than the highest tree; it was
the home of the heroes, some of whom, after their earthly
deeds, lived on as stars. The Milky Way was a path over
which the sky-people travelled, while the Sun-woman
with her fiery torch and the Moon-man with his smaller
torch gave light to all the world. The Aurora Australis

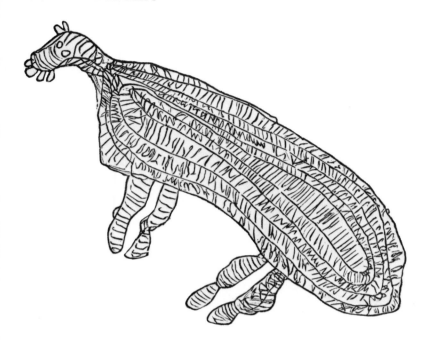

A bunyip, drawn by a River Murray Aboriginal in 1848. The bunyip, much dreaded, was believed to live in deep waterholes or swamps

was the blood shed by men fighting a great battle, and a shooting star was a medicine-man's firestick dropping to kill someone. Explanations might vary, but almost nothing was strange and impossible to understand in the heavens or on the earth. The Aborigines' task was to learn to live in harmony with the many living things that shared the world with them.

This task was made easier through belief in totemism. For Aborigines totemism brought humans and the environment together. Aborigines were not alone in this belief: the American Indians held a similar idea. In Aboriginal society individuals had their own totem, which identified them with a natural object. The members of the bandicoot totemic group, for example, believed in a special link with the bandicoot, which as their totem became their guardian. It was even more than this, for it became the symbol of common ancestry to members of that group, linking them to the Dreaming and its heroes. Each Aboriginal clan had its totem and, since the clan could also include plants and animals, a special relationship existed between its human and non-human members.

Like other matters in Aboriginal society the concept of totemism could be quite complicated. There were differences, for example, in the way totemism was observed. Sometimes a person's totem was identified by

the elders, who decided exactly what spirit-child could have entered a mother's body through a particular food she had eaten, or through her being near a totem centre at some stage. Some types of totem were inherited—a child could inherit the totem of the father's or maternal uncle's cult group. But everywhere the totems were greatly honoured, and normally Aborigines could not kill or eat their own totem animal or plant; instead, they would carry out rituals to increase its numbers. Thus totems were held in great respect. The anthropologist Herbert Basedow gave an instance of this:

I well remember on one occasion on the Alberga River I discovered a small black and yellow banded snake which I killed. An Aluridja man who was attached to the party at the time was greatly shocked at this, and, with genuine sorrow, told me that I had killed his 'brother'. Turning to an Arunndta he lamented aloud: '*Kornye! Nanni kallye nuka kalla illum,*' which literally translated means: 'Oh dear! This brother of mine is dead.'[4]

Death

Totems were vital in Aboriginal life, emphasising the close link between Aborigines and the spirit-world around them. Aborigines believed the world abounded

Uluru (Ayers Rock), Northern Territory, an important totemic site—a photo taken about 1900. 'Every precipice, cave, gutter, and mark on the top and sides of the Rock commemorates the exploits and adventures of the creatures of . . . long-distant times.'—C.P. Mountford

with spirits, some friendly, some hostile. This belief led to explanations about the origin of human life, and also helped to explain what happened at death. Death was the end of physical life only, for a dead person's spirit was then released from the body. It would make its way to a home in the sky with the spirit-ancestors, or to a spirit-centre such as a waterhole, where it could await rebirth in another human form. In some groups it was believed the spirit was carried across the sea to a land of the dead.

Death was a complex issue. Aborigines often believed there was another form of the dead person's spirit, called the 'trickster spirit'. This mischievous spirit sought to remain near the body and cause trouble. It was best not to disturb it. After mourning their loss, often with loud wailing and gashing of their bodies, the family members left the scene of death, though mourning ceremonies could still follow. To prevent arousing the trickster spirit, the use of the dead person's name was avoided for a long time, possibly for ever. But there were often visible reminders of death, such as a mound grave, a cremation

A nineteenth century engraving of huts erected over graves at the River Murray. The huts helped to ward off dingoes

*Pukamani (burial ceremony)
poles of the Tiwi people,
Northern Territory*

site, or a tree-platform on which the body was placed, together with white clay and bark armlets worn by mourners. Graveposts were often erected. In northern Australia, where funeral rituals were important and prolonged, the graveposts of the Tiwi people on Bathurst and Melville Islands were grandly decorated, and were features of the sacred (*Pukamani*) mourning ceremonies held there.

'Magic', Doctors and Cures

The death of a person neither old nor killed in fighting was a disturbing event, causing much consternation and mourning. The death, it was claimed, must be due to an enemy. This touched closely on the matter of 'magic', a powerful factor in Aboriginal life. It was believed death could be brought about by another person's 'magic'. If so, the death had to be avenged, and every effort was made to find a person who could be held responsible for it—perhaps someone who had quarrelled with the dead person or shown jealousy, or who had offended in some other way. A number of signs might identify the person to be blamed. To settle the matter, a revenge expedition could be sent out, or an agreement might be arranged with the guilty party.

The talents of Aboriginal 'doctors'—often known as 'medicine-men', though a few women also had the same role—gave further evidence of 'magical' power. These doctors, who had undertaken special initiation, directed their efforts towards curing sicknesses, finding the causes of death, making rain (or stopping it) and predicting the future. An evil spirit entering the body was believed to cause sickness, and had to be removed in order to cure the patient. Here the services of the doctors were required. A cure was attempted by rubbing or sucking the affected part. Usually the doctor managed to produce a piece of bone or stick which was claimed to have come from the sick person and to have been responsible for the malady. These doctors were often able to bring about a cure because of the psychological effect of their work, and they became greatly respected.

Minor illnesses were often treated by first-aid measures. Various plants were crushed and soaked in

A Warramunga man in traditional society, wearing a woman's head-rings as a magic cure for headache

water to provide a fluid for the relief of stomach trouble, snakebite and injuries. Blood was drawn from a patient to help relieve headaches. Tourniquets were applied to lessen pain. Heat was used to treat aches and pains, with a sick person either lying in hot sand or receiving steam treatment. Some illnesses were more difficult to cure— eye-troubles, common among a people exposed to dust and glare, were like this, and fractured limbs, although often splinted, seldom mended well.

Ceremonial Gatherings and Performers

It would be a mistake to suppose that Aboriginal life was made continually grim by sickness or sorcery. Nor did ritual duties make Aborigines over-serious and reserved. Daily life brought many simple pleasures, and Aborigines became known for their good humour and temperament. Pleasure could be found and expressed in music and dance at gatherings. Many gatherings were non-sacred occasions, without the restrictions applying to sacred ceremonies. They centred on day-to-day experiences, dramatising the affairs of humans and the natural world through singing, dancing and noise-making.

Music for simple gatherings, and for ceremonies, was easily made. Sometimes Aborigines merely slapped their thighs to make the sound. At other times, pieces of wood (such as boomerangs) were struck together to provide the rhythmic beat for dancing. Bundles of gum leaves fastened around the ankles and arms enabled Aborigines to

Aborigines at play, kicking a ball (mid-nineteenth century, S.T. Gill)

imitate the rustling of emu feathers. The most distinctive sounds were the wailing chants of the Aborigines themselves or the droning notes of the *didjeridu*, the long pipe made from a bamboo or eucalyptus branch and found in certain northern parts of Australia. A skilled blower of the *didjeridu* was not always easy to find, and a person who could blow it well, never seeming to stop for breath and capable of producing notes of two different pitches, was in great demand.

A songman, too, was highly regarded. He was a special performer who composed songs to describe day-to-day events. His extensive repertoire could be enriched by songs handed down from ancestors. Like the skilled *didjeridu* player, the songman was often asked to perform for other groups, and was paid for his services. He could be noted for his voice of varying pitch, leading others in a chorus. There were specialist leaders in dancing as well. This was a central part of ceremonies and often involved miming, especially of the actions of animals.

The Palti dance, South Australia, in the 1840s. The performers painted themselves like skeletons and made a range of gestures, shaking their legs and making a loud noise. At the end of each act there was a tremendous shout. (Illustration by G.F Angas)

The Kuri dance, being performed in South Australia in the 1840s. (G.F. Angas)

Language and Communication

Aborigines in traditional societies used artistic means of communicating feelings and ideas in their gatherings and sacred ceremonies. Speech, of course, was the normal means of communication at other times. There were a great number of different languages and dialects spoken, possibly about six hundred in all, but they had a general similarity, except perhaps for the Tasmanian ones. Because Aboriginal languages were unlike those in other countries and had apparently been spoken for a long time, it seems they developed in Australia itself. They were often rich in meaning and vocabulary, especially in reference to the natural world. To understand any of them it is necessary to understand the way their users lived and thought. Words were often built up to a considerable length, and were spoken in voices of a reasonably high pitch. In different parts of the continent variations could be noticed in the different language sounds, the use of vowels or consonants at the end of words, and so on. These variations can be recognised even now in surviving Aboriginal place names. Accents, body gestures and other mannerisms gave fuller meaning to spoken words.

Since there were so many spoken languages but no written language, it was often difficult for Aborigines to communicate beyond their own language group. Message-sticks carried when travelling had in fact no messages written on them, but were to help identify the

Two message-sticks formerly used in Western Australia

bearer and give him some authority. Sign language, used extensively, was a common method of overcoming the language difficulty. Signs were made with the hands or by facial or body movements. They could also be used within a group to convey secret meanings and to give messages when hunting. This allowed considerable 'conversations' to go on. Another form of communication was by smoke-signals—these, like message-sticks, conveyed no actual message, but were pre-arranged signs useful in hunting and in fixing a camp location. A visitor also made them to announce arrival in a strange territory.

Visual Art

Finally, there were other important ways in which Aborigines expressed themselves, ways that can be called visual art. This term refers mainly to the techniques of painting, shaping and carving, carried out on wood, bark, rock surfaces and the ground. There was also the painting of the human body for ceremonial purposes. Other forms of artistic expression, such as making designs on skin cloaks and modelling with beeswax, were uncommon. Some of the results of artistic expression, such as the richly decorated graveposts of the Tiwi people, have already been mentioned, and have become widely recognised through displays and photographs as symbols of Aboriginal life.

Aboriginal art reflected the everyday experiences of the people, but its greatest inspiration came from the sacred life, rich in its stories of the Dreaming, totemic beliefs and the spirit-world. In this kind of art Aborigines were doing more than just making representations. They were expressing their beliefs visually and linking themselves to the spirit-world. The great creation period, with its stories of ancestral beings and their deeds, was a special source of inspiration. Aboriginal art was 'sung' as much as painted or engraved, and by singing or chanting as they worked Aborigines gave their art a religious meaning. This brought them closer to the spirit-ancestors and the things in nature they wished to influence. Aboriginal art was often art with a strong purpose, art that tried to communicate ideas and not act as a kind of photograph. So an Aborigine reverently repainting sacred designs in a rockface was renewing contact with the Dreaming and reinforcing the power in the designs. An Aborigine who

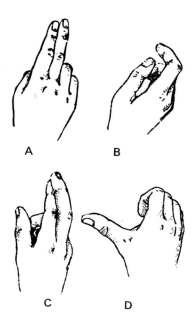

Hand signs recorded from Central Australia: Figures A and B show the signs for a small kangaroo; C, the sign for a kangaroo rat; D, the sign for an opossum

An artist making a brush for painting, Snake Bay, Melville Island

painted a representation of an emu hunt was trying to influence the result of such a hunt.

Most Aboriginal visual art is symbolic in form, and does not attempt to show exact likenesses of things. Many of its patterns and designs have thus not been understood by people from another cultural background. Aboriginal art has reserved its hidden meaning for those who have the ritual knowledge and experience to understand it. To an Aborigine, art lived. Re-tracing a painting in ochre could bring an increase in the animal and plant species in the painting, but leaving the painting unattended for a long time and allowing it to fade could lead to a failure of the rains, a decline in food, and the possibility of death.

The style and amount of visual art practised throughout the continent varied considerably. Tasmanian Aborigines in traditional society seem to have done little, for

only a few rock engravings, hand stencils and bark paintings survive. In the drier areas of the mainland art was neither extensive nor diverse, probably because the Aborigines there spent a more wandering life in search of food. Nevertheless they made rock engravings and paintings (often of geometrical design), designs on weapons, and also fine ground and body painting (often with clan symbols) for ritual purposes. Red and yellow ochres were widely traded for use in these works; white pipeclay and black charcoal were also frequently used. In eastern and southern Australia there was quite extensive art on rock surfaces. Galleries of rock engravings in some

An example of old art: an engraved spiral in the James Range, Central Australia

mountain gorges—such as in the Flinders Ranges in South Australia and in western New South Wales—show thousands of figures, featuring animals, tracks of animals and birds, patterns of circles, human figures, weapons and special designs. Eastern Australia was also noted for its many carved trees (with patterns carved into the heartwood, for burial and initiation purposes, among the Wiradjuri and Kamilaroi peoples) and for patterns on the ground ('bora grounds') for initiation ceremonies.

But it was in northern Australia that Aboriginal art really flourished. In the Kimberleys were the great rock paintings of the ancestral Wandjina figures, the spirit-ancestors responsible for rain-making. In Arnhem Land visual art, with much use of ochre, was especially fine. Here Aborigines decorated ceremonial objects, and painted and engraved on rock and bark surfaces. They left magnificent examples of their work. Notable are the ancient figure paintings of the Mimis—small spirit people painted on rockfaces in active scenes with figures from the natural environment. Examples of 'X-ray art' survive, in which animals were painted showing internal organs as well as their external outline. In Arnhem Land, too, there have been decorative bark paintings, frequently painted on the inside of bark shelters and inspired by the numerous religious cults of the area.

Many northern sites, with ancestral beings not only depicted but held to be present in spirit form, still have paintings of great age and power, and retain their sacred meaning for Aborigines. Visitors to Kakadu National Park can see rock paintings of outstanding cultural significance. At some sites—and not merely in the north of the continent—more recent paintings and engravings overlie older art, showing the use of the same sites over thousands of years. Art is another way in which traditional ideas were passed down through generations of people. But again, ideas were not static: new forms of art, and fresh subjects in the older forms, appeared. For example, representations were made of the arrival of the Macassans and of the impact of European settlement. Although the significance of some very old art has now been forgotten, Aborigines in recent times have turned with renewed vigour to artistic expression, using traditional ideas in new works. This has led to an upsurge in painting, especially since 1971 in Central and Western Australian Aboriginal settlements, where notable bark and canvas paintings have been produced.

Arnhem Land paddles decorated with a turtle design

* * *

This book so far has concentrated on traditional Aboriginal life before 1788. From 1788 the invasion of the continent by European settlers overwhelmed traditional life in many places and profoundly altered it in others. Traditional Aboriginal society had been the product of tens of thousands of years of living in Australia. Although Aboriginal society had made constant adaptations over time, it differed vastly from the kind of European society transported to Australia from 1788. The difference made it almost inevitable that a merging of the

Spirit figures painted on the Nourlangie rockface, Kakadu, Northern Territory

old and new societies would be very difficult to achieve. The Europeans were not hunter-gatherers, and made very little effort to understand Aboriginal culture. With a different economic and social system, Europeans were to prove tough competitors for the resources of the land. But it was to be not just a struggle to control resources. For the Aborigines, with their deep spiritual attachment to the land, it was to be a struggle for the soul of their country.

X-ray art—a kangaroo on a Central Arnhem Land rockface

1 Howitt, A.W. *The Native Tribes of South-East Australia*, Macmillan and Co., London, 1904, p. 737.
2 Abbie, A.A. op. cit. p. 208.
3 McCarthy, F.D. op. cit. p. 115.
4 Basedow, H.H. op. cit. p. 272.

ABORIGINES AND WHITES: THE BREAKING DOWN OF ABORIGINAL SOCIETY

4

When the first European settlers arrived in 1788 the Aborigines were the sole occupants of Australia. A hundred years later Aborigines no longer held much of the continent, and many Aboriginal groups were struggling for survival. Almost everywhere white settlement had proved overpowering. There had been no peaceful adjustment between whites and Aborigines, and the frontier between them had many times been marked in blood. Even where white settlement was sparse, traditional Aboriginal society was often strongly influenced by the presence of the new arrivals.

White people, claiming they had greater natural abilities and a higher standard of civilisation, soon justified what was happening. When they later looked backwards on their short time in Australia, they began to revere the achievements of pioneering whites. The achievements of the Aboriginal people, and the story of what had happened between whites and Aborigines, were ignored or quickly passed over.

The European Explorers

Before 1788 the Macassan seamen were not the only visitors to Australia's shores. European explorers, especially the Dutch, began to make contact with Australia's coasts in the seventeenth century. The Dutch, making their way from their Indonesian trading posts, were probably the first white people Aborigines had seen. Contacts between them were very limited, for the Dutch made only fleeting visits to the coastline and had been instructed to be careful in any contacts with people found there—possibilities of trade must not be spoiled. The Dutch went back, however, from their visits to report

You will moreover go ashore in various places and diligently examine the coast in order to ascertain whether or no it is inhabited, the nature of the land and the people, their towns and inhabited villages, the divisions of their kingdoms, their religion and policy, their wars, their rivers, the shape of their vessels, their fisheries, commodities and manufactures, but specially to inform yourselves what minerals, such as gold, silver, tin, iron, lead, and copper, what precious stones, pearls, vegetables, animals and fruits, these lands yield and produce.
J.E. Heeres: *The Part Borne by the Dutch in the Discovery of Australia* 1606–1765, London, 1899, p. 19

Instructions issued in 1622 to two Dutch ships heading for the Australian coast

An artist's impression of the arrival of European ships in Australian waters—the ships of Torres, north of Australia early in the seventeenth century

that there was no chance of trade, for the land seemed miserable and full of flies. The Aborigines, unimpressed with the trinkets shown to them, resented the visitors, who had attempted to kidnap some of them. Fear, hostility and occasional bloodshed marked contact between the two sides.

In 1688 and 1699 the buccaneering Englishman William Dampier visited Australia's north-west coast. He gave Europeans a more detailed version of Aboriginal life. Without other versions to compare them with, Dampier's views became widely known and accepted. His lack of understanding led him to a disgust of Aboriginal life, influencing others to a similar conclusion. His description helped to establish the typical beliefs and attitudes—the stereotypes—that future white people were to hold about Aborigines. After Dampier it was some time before other navigators had much contact with Aborigines. The famous Englishman Lieutenant James Cook was the most important. After examining Australia's eastern coast in 1770, Cook wrote more favourably about the Aboriginal inhabitants:

... they may appear to some to be the most wretched people upon Earth, but in reality they are far more happier than we Europeans; being wholly unacquainted not only with the superfluous but the necessary Conveniences so much sought after in Europe, they are happy in not knowing the use of them ... The Earth and sea of their own accord furnishes them with all things necessary for life ...[1]

The inhabitants of this country are the miserablest people in the world. The Hodmadods of Monomatapa, though a nasty people, yet for wealth are gentlemen to these; who have no houses and skin garments, sheep, poultry, and fruits of the earth, ostrich eggs, etc., as the Hodmadods have; and setting aside their human shape, they differ but little from brutes. They are tall, straight-bodied and thin, with small, long limbs. They have great heads, round foreheads, and great brows. Their eye-lids are always half closed, to keep the flies out of their eyes, they being so troublesome here that no fanning will keep them from coming to one's face . . . So that, from their infancy, being thus annoyed with these insects, they do never open their eyes as other people do; and therefore they cannot see far, unless they hold up their heads as if they were looking at somewhat over them.

They have great bottle-noses, pretty full lips and wide mouths, the two fore-teeth of their upper jaw are wanting in all of them, men and women, old and young: neither have they any beards. They are long-visaged, and of a very unpleasing aspect, having no one graceful feature in their faces. Their hair is black, short, and curled, like that of the negroes; and not long and lank . . . The colour of their skins, both of their faces and the rest of their body, is coal black, like that of the negroes of Guinea.

They have no sort of clothes, but the piece of the rind of a tree ty'd lyke a girdle about their waists, and a handful of long grass, or three or four small green boughs, full of leaves, thrust under their girdle to cover their nakedness.

They have no houses, but lye in the open air without any covering the earth being their bed and the heaven their canopy. Whether they cohabit one to one woman, or promiscuously, I know not. But they do live in companies, twenty or thirty men, women and children together. Their only food is a small sort of fish, which they get by making wares of stone across little coves or branches of the sea; every tide bringing in the little fish, and there leaving them a prey to these people, who constantly attend there to search at low water.

. . . I did not perceive that they did worship anything. These poor creatures have a sort of weapon to defend their ware or fight with their enemies, if they have any that will interfere with their poor fishery. They did endeavour with their weapons to frighten us who, lying ashore, deterr'd them from one of their fishing places. Some of them had wooden swords, others had a sort of lances. The sword is a piece of wood shaped somewhat like a cutlass. The lance is a long strait pole, sharp at one end, and hardened afterwards by heat. I saw no iron, nor any other sort of metal; therefore it is probable they use stone hatchets . . .

How they get their fire I know not but probably, as Indians do, out of wood.

Invasion

Captain Arthur Phillip and the First Fleet reached Botany Bay in 1788. Their arrival began what is now often regarded as the European invasion of Australia. Phillip had been instructed to make friendly contact with the Aborigines. He was not only to ensure peaceful relations with them but see whether they could become useful in the first settlement. But Aboriginal land rights were completely ignored. Captain Cook had already laid claim to

Part of William Dampier's description of the Aborigines on the north-west coast of Australia. (After the account in his New Voyage Round the World *1697)*

eastern Australia for Britain, and in 1788 Britain simply claimed sovereignty over the eastern part of the continent. Britain considered it now owned this huge part of Australia. The land was judged to be 'waste and unoccupied' and the British thus regarded the First Fleet as bringing the first colonists to Australia. This was the basis on which Britain established the first and the later settlements, openly denying any Aboriginal title to the land and claiming to be supplying the first settlers on the land. When it was found that Aborigines did not appear to fence and cultivate the land but seemed to simply wander over it, British possession was considered to be further justified.

The Aborigines showed surprise and some resentment at their first sight of the new arrivals. Men brandished their spears and women and children often hid. The whites were feared as the returning spirits of the dead. But Aborigines did not mount a strong resistance to the founding of the convict colony. For his part, Governor Phillip tried to secure friendly relations with the Aborigines near the first settlement. He had an unusual advantage in his task, since his missing front tooth was a sign of status to Aborigines.

Troubles, however, soon began, as white settlement obviously became more permanent. Manners and customs were different. While some people in Europe at the time believed in a certain nobility about the quality of life in more 'primitive' societies, and thus spoke about the 'noble savage', convicts and others in the Sydney district began to treat Aborigines as less than noble savages. Aboriginal ways were thought to be uncivilised, and there was no understanding of the organised social system of the Aboriginal people, with its religious background. Soon physical clashes occurred. Fearful whites wanted Aborigines to keep away from their settlements.

Phillip was anxious for Aborigines to tell him more about the inland districts. Even after he was wounded by a spear he kept his desire to befriend Aborigines. This gave way to exasperation when his personal huntsman was speared; he demanded blood and a revenge expedition. Phillip seemed puzzled by the Aborigines, and was disappointed that whites could not 'civilise' them. Aborigines were unattracted by European ways, although one man—Bennelong—accompanied Governor Phillip on his return to England and easily adopted European clothes, manners, speech—and liquor. Other Aborigines

In the morning of the 27th our men went ashore again for the purpose of attempting to get hold of one or two natives, but did not succeed in doing so that day, because they landed too late to lure the natives to the beach. Early in the morning of the 28th they again landed in order to execute their plan; on their arrival the natives came up to them dancing and singing, sat down close to them, laid aside their so-called assagays or weapons, and again enjoyed the liquor with which our men plied them. While they were thus making merry, our men seized hold of two of them, upon which the others jumped to their feet, snatched up their assagays and began to throw them at our people without, however, wounding any one; except that the ship's clerk, who in flying tried to seize one of the natives round the body, was in the scuffle slightly wounded in the hand; upon this our men fired a volley, wounding one of the natives, who thereupon all of them fled into the bush.
J.E. Heeres: op. cit., p. 94.

in the Sydney district, often led by the noted warrior Pemulwuy and later his son Tedbury, began a fierce resistance to the white invasion. For years Pemulwuy's spirited opposition disturbed European settlements. The belief even grew—until he was shot in 1802 and his head sent to England—that he could not be harmed by bullets.

White officials and settlers became disillusioned as well as fearful. Although Governor Lachlan Macquarie later tried to help the 'civilising' process by establishing an Aboriginal school at Parramatta and a farm at Port Jackson, many whites began to believe that little could be done to 'civilise' Aborigines. They thought it did not matter if Aborigines began to die out as a race, and that tough methods had to be used to stop continued clashes between the two groups. These clashes became increasingly common along the margin of settlement where, if government protection was not available, white settlers took matters into their own hands.

See opposite:
An incident involving a Dutch exploring party on Cape York Peninsula in 1756

Differences and Racial Clash

Aborigines in early Sydney and other districts could see little point in many European practices. They did not need to cultivate the soil or keep domesticated animals, since the natural environment provided for their wants. Similarly they saw little need for European learning and religion—they had their own skills and their own explanations of the world around them. In fact Aborigines often proved the better teachers. They showed white settlers the trees that provided the best timbers for various purposes and how to cut and treat bark for hut making; they showed how to obtain bark fibre, valuable for rope, and other skills. Above all Aborigines proved excellent guides, especially to white explorers, in strange country.

The whites claimed that physical clashes occurred because Aborigines were naturally wicked and loved fighting. The claim was not accurate. Aborigines in their own society were a peaceful people. Fighting among them was usually on a limited scale, often stopping when the first blood was drawn. There was nothing like the wars known among European people for territory, nor did Aborigines form large-scale combinations for fighting. And Aborigines could scarcely have been impressed by what they saw among the new arrivals, for convict

PIPER.

An illustration published in 1836 of Piper, who accompanied Major Mitchell on an exploring expedition

society offered daily examples of harshness and ill-treatment.

White people also claimed that Aborigines had no idea of land ownership, therefore white settlers could not be dispossessing them. Why, they asked, did Aborigines resent the new arrivals so much?

Part of the answer was already apparent to Governor King, who became governor of New South Wales in 1800. He realized that loss of land was a major reason for trouble, although settlers continued to claim Aborigines had no land of their own. Whites would not learn from the example of Bennelong, the Aborigine they knew best, who repeatedly declared that the island of Me-mul (Goat Island), near Sydney Cove, was his own and his family's home. Like other Aborigines Bennelong was deeply attached to his land.[2] To be forced from their group land meant that Aborigines lost their spiritual homes as well as their source of food. In occupying Aboriginal land, whites drove off game, destroyed vegetation, fouled waterholes and showed no respect for sacred places. A modern writer, Professor Colin Tatz, has shown the nature of what was happening:

For Aborigines . . . land is a spiritual thing, a phenomenon from which culture and religion derive. It is not sellable or buyable. Land is not private property . . . Land was and is endowed with a magical quality, involving a relationship to the sun and the water and the earth and the animals all put together—for the collective use of all. The notion of a fence to separate portions of the land was unknown to them, for fences defaced the land. They could not, and some still cannot, understand the concept of making land into private property and giving its 'owners' the right to bar everyone else . . . And so bloody conflict and massacre developed . . . because whites 'took' what Aborigines did not comprehend could be 'taken'.[3]

As white settlement spread after 1800, clashes continued. Officials in Britain and New South Wales thought the matter was simple. The British Crown was held to own the land. People of both races inhabiting the land were claimed to be British subjects. Aborigines were neither consulted nor given a choice. They were actually declared to be under the protection of the law, but this proved little. In fact whites were those who clamoured for protection and who received it most. With the wool

*See opposite:
Two scenes of Aborigines at Botany Bay, published in the* Voyage of Governor Phillip to Botany Bay *(1789). In these exaggerated scenes the Aborigines are pictured as 'noble savages', at a time when whites regarded them favourably. (Compare illustrations in the following pages, where later artists obviously had different feelings)*

An Aboriginal rock painting depicting the coming of Europeans

trade becoming more prosperous, settlers then began settling on new grazing land after the Blue Mountains were crossed. In more distant areas official protection of either race was more difficult and often not attempted. Violence—'guerilla warfare'—extended again along the frontier of settlement. Guns were at the ready, or were used, on many pastoral properties. Aborigines, too, took to arms, using spears against settlers and stock. Inevitably, clashes ended in the taking of Aboriginal land and the subjection of the people.

The nature of relations between Aborigines and Europeans varied in different districts and was not always violent. European diseases were often the most destructive agent in the decline of Aboriginal groups. Surviving Aborigines began to live in towns as well as country areas. European missionaries sought to break down Aboriginal beliefs and convert Aborigines to Christianity, but they also tried to provide some relief to suffering Aborigines. Yet by the 1830s relationships between Europeans and Aborigines were at a critical stage.

See opposite: Aborigines in New South Wales drinking bool *or sugar water, and Aborigines fighting in Sydney. These scenes, by Charles Rodius in about 1836, reveal as much about how white settlers regarded Aborigines as they do about the actual condition of Aborigines near white settlements at the time*

European settlers had seized great stretches of country in New South Wales. Some pitched battles and other incidents were of major significance. In northern New South Wales in 1838 a group of station-hands killed twenty-eight bound Aborigines in what became known as the Myall Creek Massacre. In this case, unlike many others, the seven station-hands held to be responsible were convicted and hanged for their crime, despite white sympathy for them. Many whites seemed to share the view of a writer a little earlier: 'Speaking of them collectively, it must be confessed I entertain very little more respect for the aborigines of New Holland, than for the ourang-outang . . .' They would have shared his further opinion: 'We have taken possession of their country, and are determined to keep it . . .'[4]

The Other Colonies

In Van Diemen's Land the position was even worse. In 1804, soon after white settlement began, some 'innocent and well disposed' Aborigines were murdered at Risdon Cove, starting a chain reaction of unpleasant incidents. Lawless sealers and convicts, in murdering Aborigines and kidnapping Aboriginal women, provoked Aborigines to hatred and a desire for revenge. The settlers wanted to solve the Aboriginal question decisively; some simply wanted to exterminate all Aborigines on the island. They looked to the governor, Lieut.-Colonel Arthur, to take strong action. After several futile measures, Arthur tried to outlaw Aborigines from the settled districts. Soon he declared martial law and began in 1830 an amazing military operation, in which five thousand whites attempted to drive the remaining Aborigines into the Tasman Peninsula. This so-called 'Black War', said to be extremely costly, failed dismally—only two Aborigines were captured. It was left to George Robinson, a bricklayer of simple faith, to attempt a government policy of conciliation. Making contact with surviving groups, he persuaded Aborigines to make their home on Flinders Island. Though this provided some physical safety, Aborigines now lacked the spiritual comfort of their own lands. Urged to accept strange European customs and learning, Tasmania's Aborigines continued to decline in numbers. By 1850 few survived.

In Western Australia, settled in the 1820s, the early aims of protecting Aborigines and offering them the

A wordless proclamation, issued by Governor Arthur in Van Diemen's Land in 1828, to discourage fighting between whites and Aborigines

benefits of European learning and religion were, as elsewhere, soon outweighed by other concerns. Governor Stirling allowed whites to take strong measures against Aborigines said to be causing trouble. Stirling personally took part in the 'Battle of Pinjarra' to punish Aborigines of the Murray River district south of Perth. Once again the Aborigines faced strong pressure from whites determined to occupy the land and use arms if they chose.

At Port Phillip Bay in 1835 an initial attempt was made at land negotiations. John Batman, an ambitious pastoralist from Van Diemen's Land, was anxious to secure good grazing land near the Yarra for himself and his partners. Unable to win official approval to settle there, Batman simply bargained with local Aborigines for a large

Tasmanian Aboriginal women in the 1860s, showing the obvious influence of European contact

Wybalenna, the settlement at Flinders Island in 1847. This was one of the early institutions set up for Aborigines

tract of land. The New South Wales governor declared this private treaty illegal, and although settlement at Port Phillip expanded quickly and profitably for other whites, Batman obtained no benefit from his curious deal. Nor did Aborigines, who soon found their traditional life decaying and their numbers declining. This was despite the appointment of official protectors of Aborigines, the founding of mission stations and schools, and an attempt to form a 'Native Police' force which recruited Aborigines themselves for police work.

Great hopes were held that South Australia, settled in 1836, would be free of the racial troubles elsewhere. In Britain officials influenced by the humanitarian movement of the time were anxious to give South Australia's Aborigines much greater protection and the blessings of British ways and the Christian religion. They believed South Australia could be a model colony in this respect. Although a protector of Aborigines was appointed and although a good deal of humanitarian talk about kindly treatment took place, efforts and results were feeble. The Kaurna people around Adelaide was soon shattered as a unit. Aboriginal groups surviving longer felt limited benefit from occasional educational, missionary and welfare attempts. Far from being a model colony in its relations with Aborigines, South Australia resembled the other colonies in the rapid occupation of Aboriginal lands, the physical violence between the races, and the settlers' ignorance of the nature of Aboriginal society. And once again the original idea of giving protection to

A group of Aborigines, showing the obvious influence of European contact, in South Australia about 1850

Aborigines soon gave way to settlers' demands for protection from Aborigines, especially after clashes involving
overlanders bringing stock to South Australia.

In northern Australia Aborigines and whites engaged
in an often violent struggle in the Moreton Bay district
(part of the future colony of Queensland). White settlers
often resorted to poisoned food and guns along the very
troubled frontier. As settlement advanced, the Native
Police force—used before in Victoria and New South
Wales—became prominent. These mounted Aboriginal
troopers, enlisted from remote districts to use their skills
of bushcraft against their own race, were trained to en-
force peace ruthlessly as pastoral holdings were developed. For whites, the possession of potentially valuable
grazing land in the Darling Downs and other areas was
at stake; for local Aborigines, this was traditional land
and the lifeblood of their existence. Only on stations
where their labour was valued were Aborigines welcome;
elsewhere they were likely to be attacked indiscriminate-
ly. In the Northern Territory things were no better. From
the time of John McDouall Stuart's explorations, the
Northern Territory was a scene of racial conflict, a conflict
marked by mistrust and violence in which guns, spears
and staghounds often featured. Administrators made
only feeble efforts to calm the situation. Matters were left
to the settlers themselves or entrusted to police leading
punitive expeditions and forces of Native Police. Cattle
spearing would often be the reason given for such an expedition, frequently leading to loss of Aboriginal lives.

The Impact of Settlement

Such actions hastened the decline of Aboriginal groups
during the nineteenth century, though the decline went
on even where there was friendship and trust on both
sides. The decline came despite the setting up of government ration-stations to distribute flour and blankets to
needy Aborigines, and despite the work of missionary es-
tablishments and official protectors of Aborigines. It
came, too, despite the often spirited resistance of Aboriginal people to the seizure of their land and the attacks
on their culture.

The land question lay at the heart of the decline of
traditional Aboriginal society. The declared attitude of the
British and colonial governments remained clear: the

land, 'waste and uncultivated', belonged to the whites, even if they had not yet occupied parts of it. Even where some land reserves were set aside for Aborigines, the colonial governments claimed actual ownership of the reserves and white pastoralists could often graze their stock there. Only a few whites admitted that Aborigines were being dispossessed of their land.

Two groups of white squatters, as sketched by a young Aborigine in the nineteenth century

The Aboriginal people regarded white settlement as an unjustified intrusion on their lands. Sheep and cattle began to eat out the native grasses and drive off the game which provided essential meat food. The situation was made worse by the white pastoralists' determination to control the existing waterholes, soon fouled by stock. There was an increasing upset in the balance between Aboriginal population numbers and the available food supply. The white intruders showed no desire to compensate, and did not acknowledge the food-sharing practices found among the Aboriginal people themselves. The situation, of course, was not simply an economic one, since whites and their stock were occupying sacred Aboriginal places, such as the totemic sites to which Aborigines were reverently attached.

It was little wonder that Aborigines began their own campaign of spirited resistance on the frontier of settlement. They speared stock which were on their hunting-grounds and which they thus believed they were entitled to hunt. In many areas a bitter racial conflict began, in which Aborigines were at a disadvantage in arms, especially when whites could make greater use of rifles in the latter part of the nineteenth century. The first interest of white governments came to be to provide protection *from* the Aborigines, rather than *of* them. Police action, punitive raids and legal enforcement were some of the methods used. It is no exaggeration to conclude that actual warfare thus took place over a long period in Australia.

One Law for All

In legal proceedings Aborigines were at a considerable disadvantage. Because Aborigines were regarded as incapable of understanding the oath in European courts, their evidence was not accepted. When this situation was later corrected, Aborigines were still greatly disadvantaged. No Aborigine appeared as prosecutor, juror or judge. Court procedures and the legal code were European, and bewildering to Aborigines. Translation of Aboriginal languages caused problems in court, and Aboriginal customs and law were not taken into account. The position was made worse by the Aboriginal tendency to look for, and give, the answer required by the prosecution. Aborigines also became victims of bias and prejudice in courts, which were anxious to uphold white dominance and did not acknowledge Aboriginal title to the land. The punishment system made matters far worse—its basis was not understood and it left Aborigines confused and very fearful.

The Europeans' failure to consider Aboriginal law and customs was part of the pattern of white supremacy. This made no allowance for Aboriginal practices. In traditional society, of course, Aborigines were bound by strict obligations and codes of conduct, which whites simply refused to recognise. Aborigines settled disputes by different means, involving actual or ceremonial punishments and not detention. The idea was to restore normal group life as quickly as possible. Whites were unwilling or unable to understand the Aboriginal system. They failed to observe obligations which Aborigines thought should apply to whites as well as themselves. This caused much Aboriginal resentment—especially the practice of whites trespassing on Aboriginal land and the troubles arising from the whites' desire for relationships with Aboriginal women.

The Breakdown of Aboriginal Society

As white colonists seized Aboriginal land—land with its spiritual as well as economic importance—there began the assault on traditional Aboriginal society. Beliefs, social customs and morale were weakened as Aboriginal numbers declined. No longer did the social system firmly support Aboriginal groups; ritual duties were no longer performed with the old vigour. The spiritual basis of Aboriginal life was undermined.

The whites' desire to educate and convert Aborigines hastened the breakdown of Aboriginal society. Whites usually described that society as primitive. Aboriginal beliefs and customs were ridiculed, as attempts were made to replace them with European culture. This culture puzzled rather than satisfied Aborigines, to whom it had little relevance. Aborigines found adjustment difficult. Their own world was one in which tradition was highly

Aborigines' Mia Mia, New South Wales, taken by Charles Kerry in the 1890s

important—unlike whites, they placed no emphasis on change. In turn Aborigines were criticised for their apparent unwillingness to live according to 'civilised' ways. Meanwhile Aboriginal social life continued to decline. White missionaries, by discouraging initiation ceremonies, hindered younger Aborigines from being accepted as full participants in traditional life. Whites encouraged Aboriginal marriages which cut across traditional kinship rules. Other patterns of behaviour, so important in regulating Aboriginal social life, decayed.

White settlers usually concentrated on the material problems of colonial life. In the clash for land, especially in remote parts, the settlers' fear of Aborigines was noticeable. The Aborigines seemed part of a strange land with distinctive fauna. (Aborigines were even described as 'wild' or 'tame', while the term 'savages' survived from early days.) Then, after the stage of clash between the races, came the decline of Aboriginal traditional life.

Camp of Australian Aborigines: taken in 1895 in the Grafton district, New South Wales, by G.W. Wilson

The Ilbalintja soak has been defiled by the hands of white men. Two white men came here to sink a well. They put down into the sacred soak plugs of gelignite, to blast an opening through the hard rock at the bottom. But the rock was too hard for them. They had to leave without having been able to shatter it; they took ill soon afterwards and died.

And now the soak has almost gone dry. No longer do men pluck up the grass and the weeds and sweep the ground clean around it; no longer do they care for the resting place of Karora. Bushes have grown up on the very edge of the soak, and there is no one to uproot them. The bandicoots have vanished from the tall grass in the mulga thicket. Our young men do no longer care for the traditions of their fathers; and their women bear no children. Soon the men of Ilbalintja will be no more; we shall all sleep in our graves as our forefathers do now.

There is little here for strangers to see; there is no mountain cave here, only a storehouse in a mulga tree. But though the soak has been forsaken by almost all our people, a few of us old men still care for it. It still holds me fast; and I shall tend it while I can: while I live, I shall love to gaze on this ancient soil.

T.G.H. Strehlow; *Aranda Traditions*, Melbourne, 1947, p. 31

An Aranda man's sorrow about what had happened to a sacred site

With their control of the land gone, Aborigines drifted to the edge of towns, pastoral stations and mission stations, attracted by European material items and by food, drink, and tobacco. Hand-outs of ration food and clothing were periodically made, emphasising the unfortunate and dependent state to which Aborigines had been reduced. The availability of alcohol and tobacco began to take a severe toll of Aboriginal health.

Disease

Disease played a vital role in the breakdown of traditional Aboriginal societies. In fact introduced diseases have often been suggested as the major cause of the disappearance of many Aboriginal groups, with a much greater impact than physical violence or any other factor. Before the Macassan visits and the arrival of Europeans, Aborigines had been relatively free from diseases, their chief trouble coming from eye and skin complaints. The marsupials they hunted did not transmit their diseases to humans. But after the coming of other peoples and their stock, Aborigines began to suffer badly from the new diseases, to which they had no natural resistance. Smallpox, tuberculosis, venereal diseases and leprosy had disastrous effects, while milder diseases such as influenza, measles, whooping-cough and the common cold could be just as deadly to a people with no previous contact with them. Several descriptions stated that in some areas most, or all, of the children died from disease.

Diseases in fact often drastically reduced a local Aboriginal population even before the full pressure of white settlement was felt there. Smallpox destroyed the majority of Aborigines close to Sydney within three years of white settlement in 1788. The disease spread down the Murray to South Australia, shattering the health and numbers of Aborigines as it went. The 'smallpox song' that Aborigines sang was powerless to stop the deadly disease. The death of the traditional Aboriginal 'doctors' and the destruction of medicinal herbs by introduced stock removed the traditional Aboriginal sources of relief from illnesses. By 1850 the results of disease were already being felt in the settled areas of southern Australia, where whites were noticing the decline in the Aboriginal population. Disease robbed Aboriginal people of their spirit and ability to survive. By reducing numbers it broke down the strength of the kinship system and the links between the generations. The birth rate was lowered. Surviving groups were left unable to carry on in the former manner as strong social units. The impact of disease on the social structure of Aboriginal groups and on total numbers was profound.

'Soothing the Dying Pillow'

As the rapid decline in Aboriginal population took place, few whites tried to suggest reasons. One who did so in 1886 described the grim process and some of its causes:

Experience shows that a populous town will kill out the tribes which live near enough to visit it daily in from two to ten years ... In more sparsely-settled country the process is somewhat different and more gradual, but it leads to the same end. In the bush many tribes have disappeared, and the rest are disappearing. Towns destroy by drunkenness and debauchery; in the country, from fifteen to five-and-twenty per cent fall by the rifle; the tribe then submits, and diseases of European origin complete the process of extermination.[5]

This description showed a general pattern. The process varied in intensity according to districts, and was slowed by the efforts of a few determined whites to help Aborigines. Not all the Aboriginal groups died out. But long before 1900 most whites thought it was only a matter of time before the Aboriginal people ceased to exist. This apparent dying-out of the whole race helped to end earlier ideas—held mostly by whites in towns—about Aboriginal assimilation into the white community. Instead a different approach was suggested. Its goal was to make the passing of the Aborigines as peaceful as possible. The approach was termed 'soothing the dying pillow'. To those who cared, the policy seemed a worthy one, though it was also a policy of despair. As early as 1868, when more than three-quarters of Victoria's Aborigines

A Ngarrindjeri camp (Lower Murray district of South Australia) about 1880, showing traditional and European items

had already died out, a Melbourne editor summed up the
policy:

Let us make their passage to the grave as comfortable as
possible—let us do our best to civilize them and convert them
to Christianity; but let us not flatter ourselves that, up to the
present at any rate, we have succeeded. Something may be
done with the half-castes, but the case of the full-blooded
aboriginal is, we fear, hopeless.[6]

Whites tended to make a fuss of the last Aboriginal
members of a group, just as they did of those they described as 'king' or 'queen' of a particular group. In practice, however, few whites, or their governments, did
much towards Aboriginal welfare. Mission stations and
government reserves became the enforced homes of
many surviving Aborigines, where they were supplied
with medicine, shelter, a minimum of food, and the customary blankets. Some schooling and elementary training
in practical skills could also be provided. Governments
favoured this policy of segregation, declaring that it
would enable Aborigines to avoid contact with the worst
of the whites. Yet by encouraging the isolation of Aborigines this policy also enabled white society to avoid
Aborigines and the 'problem' of Aboriginal welfare. The
idea of 'soothing the dying pillow' was easy to accept,
for it helped to satisfy the few whites who were concerned about the Aborigines' position. It also left other
whites free to pursue their own tasks on the land taken
from Aborigines.

The Protection Policies

By 1901 Aborigines had lost control over their land in all
except the remote parts of the continent. They were not
given the chance to determine their own future. Their
culture was not respected. Aboriginal languages were
dying out with the people. Few whites took the trouble
to learn anything about Aboriginal life; many whites
regarded Aborigines as oddities or nuisances. Along the
frontier the view was still usually the same—'Bullocks
and blacks won't mix'.

It was hoped that the establishment of the new federal
government, in 1901, would lead to a better deal for
Aborigines. There were even suggestions that the new

government, and not the separate states, should have responsibility for Aboriginal affairs. But things changed little. It was decided, for example, that Aborigines should not be counted in the federal census. Thus the original owners of the land were officially not counted or regarded as Australians. The federal government had no new views on Aboriginal affairs, which remained the responsibility of the individual states. State laws reflected the desire to restrict and segregate Aborigines. A Queensland Act in 1897 set the pattern. It gave the official protectors of Aborigines wide powers to control the lives of the Aboriginal and part-Aboriginal people. It provided for reserves on which Aborigines should live and supervised their movements and employment by whites. Western Australia and South Australia adopted similar legislation, so that Aborigines who no longer lived in their traditional societies often had to live on reserves under government administration. In effect they had to live as inmates of institutions.

The basis, then, of the protection policy was restriction of the Aboriginal people and their rights. As before, there was no attempt to consider what Aborigines themselves might want. Once again whites assumed that the best policy for Aborigines was to adopt white ways. If Aborigines did not follow that path, then it was said they were lacking in ability. There was always the feeling that the Aborigines, not the whites, were responsible for any failure.

Further Trouble in the North

Along the frontier of settlement in the early twentieth century, relations between whites and Aborigines continued to reveal conflict and inhumanity. In outlying areas of the Northern Territory and Western Australia some settlers and bushmen were accustomed to shoot Aborigines on sight or turn their dogs loose at sundown. Several of the worst incidents were described by Dr W.E. Roth, who was asked to make a report to the Western Australian government in 1905. He revealed 'a most brutal and outrageous state of affairs' in the northern part of the state: there was police corruption in administering Aboriginal ration allowances; the chaining together (by the neck) of arrested Aborigines and Aboriginal witnesses and prisoners; forced labour for Aboriginal children, and

heavy sentences for children and adults convicted of killing cattle; discrimination in court proceedings; and a
shortage of food.[7]

Whites in the north did not hide their fierce determination to seize and hold the land. This brought them into
opposition with some city-dwellers, who questioned not
the northerners' right to the land but the means used to
obtain it. Arguments over the issue sometimes flared in
the press. The northerners' feelings were clear, as shown
in a poem written by one of their supporters:

The civic merchant, snugly housed and fed,
Who sleeps each night on soft and guarded bed,
Who never leaves the city's beaten tracks,
May well believe in kindness to the blacks.
But he can never know, nor hardly guess,
The dangers of the pathless wilderness;
The rage and frenzy in the squatter's brain

*An Aboriginal chain gang,
about 1900, going to work
at Wyndham, Western
Australia. The guard is on
the extreme right*

*A police party with
prisoners wearing neck
chains, Ellery Creek,
MacDonnell Ranges,
Northern Territory, about
1900*

When the speared bullocks dot the spreading plain;
The lust for vengeance in the stockman's heart
Who sees his horse lie slain by savage dart;
The nervous thrill the lonely traveller feels
When round his camp the prowling savage steals;
Nor that fierce hate with which the soul is filled
When man must slaughter or himself be killed.

Ah! who shall judge? Not you, my city friend,
Whose life is free from all that can offend;
Who pass your days in comfort, ease, and peace,
Guarded by metropolitan police.
Ah! who shall judge the bushman's hasty crime
Both justified by circumstance and clime.
Could you, my friend, 'neath such assaults be still,
And never feel that wild desire to kill?
Steps in your own defence would you not take
When law is absent then your own laws make.[8]

Aboriginal stockmen branding cattle at Sturt Creek, Northern Territory, about 1900

From 1911, when it took over the administration of the Northern Territory from South Australia, the Commonwealth became more involved in Aboriginal affairs. Its policy of protection resembled the policy found in several of the states. Every aspect of Aboriginal life was carefully regulated. The Aborigines' freedom of movement was greatly restricted. For many Aborigines, life became centred on institutions established under government control, where the opportunity to make personal decisions and live in simple dignity was slight. Special conditions governed their employment, while their personal property remained under the control of the government's chief protector of Aborigines. The protector, not the children's parents, was the legal guardian of the children.

Yet the Commonwealth was no more able than the states to improve Aboriginal affairs. The Northern Territory remained prone to racial disturbances, which police solved as they saw fit. In places such as Arnhem Land it was possible for Aborigines to lead a better life, in more traditional manner. But around white settlements and stations Aborigines camped in poverty, valued only when their labour was essential in the pastoral industry. The Commonwealth seemed to forget they existed, until their condition came to public notice late in the 1920s. At that time drought threatened natural food supplies, bringing concern in southern cities about the Aborigines' plight. About another matter—the 'Coniston Massacre'—there were louder complaints. Following the death in 1928 of a white prospector at Coniston Station in Central Australia, a police expedition set out to find the culprits. In a series of raids police took heavy toll of Aboriginal lives. The reaction from city people interested in Aboriginal welfare was hostile, and not softened by an official report justifying the raids and the police shooting of many Aborigines. Reports of killings elsewhere, such as in the Kimberleys, and of the miserable conditions which many Aborigines were forced to endure, aroused further concern.

Such troubles revived the arguments between whites in towns and those on the edge of settlement about policies towards Aborigines. Like others earlier, there were settlers who still thought and spoke of Aborigines as a kind of animal, describing them as 'wild' or 'tame'. Many whites still took refuge in the belief that the Aboriginal race was dying out, despite evidence to the contrary. Even as late as 1938 Daisy Bates, the well-known worker for the Aborigines on the Nullarbor, published her book under the title of *The Passing of the Aborigines*.

Malnutrition

Malnutrition and disease continued to play havoc with Aboriginal health as the twentieth century wore on. A white doctor, well informed about the Aboriginal situation, even claimed later that malnutrition was the greatest damage inflicted by the whites and the one least acknowledged with regret.[9] Government and station rations were often inadequate. Flour, sugar and tea were the basic rations, following the pattern laid down in the

Distributing rations to Aborigines in South Australia, 1913

. . . I have lived at . . . Mission Stations, for a few years, until I could live there no longer owing to the high cost of living, and the very poor wages . . . ranging from 5/- to 7/- per day for married men with families . . . I can hardly make both ends meet on . . . 14/- per day, but by going out shearing or doing other piece work or contract work I seem to manage. Rations and blankets to the aged and needy are of inferior quality, one blanket for two married adults, rations unrefined sugar, second rate flour and last grade tea. These are only supplied to the aged full-blooded Aboriginal, and those in dire circumstances, otherwise nil, and about land or farms, there should be numerous reserves all over the state, but after inquiries and applications to the Chief Protector of Aborigines for a grant of land to which we are entitled by Act of Parliament, I have been informed that certain reserves that I have applied for, do not exist as reserves which means that they have been sold. I suppose there are many like myself who would be only too glad to get a block of land on which to maintain themselves, but the Government will not give us a chance . . .

Part of a letter written by William Taylor, a South Australian Aborigine, in 1924, revealing his discontent with mission employment and the chance of obtaining land

previous century, when governments saw feeding-stations as a means of preventing Aboriginal hunger and thus possibly of preventing the spearing of stock. The absence of protein foods affected Aboriginal health and contributed to high infant mortality. Damp clothing and poor housing brought further suffering. Disease, especially tuberculosis, remained widespread and often fatal.

Some Signs of Change

On the frontier of settlement the labour question, rather than malnutrition and disease, was much discussed. But there were other problems in the 1930s. Reports came of incidents in the Northern Territory in which Aborigines along the Arnhem Land and nearby coasts clashed with Japanese adventurers searching for pearls and trepang. Peaceful relations were often disrupted by arguments about Aboriginal women, and violence followed. In one incident at Caledon Bay in 1933 five Japanese were killed. In other incidents Aboriginal and white lives were lost. Uneasiness emerged over how white missionaries were affecting Aboriginal culture in various parts of Australia, and whether Aboriginal law should be taken into account in white law courts. Opposition also emerged to the expeditions of punishment, the ill-treatment of Aboriginal witnesses, and the bias of white courts.

In southern Australia Aborigines suffered as well. Conditions on reserves, mission stations and at the edge of towns were usually squalid. The lingering ideas of segregation emphasised separating Aborigines yet still imposed forms of supervision and restriction. Aborigines had little chance of achieving the same standards of education, health and employment as whites, and prejudice against them survived strongly. Yet the supposed dying-out of the Aboriginal race did not take place. The states began to make part-Aborigines, increasing in numbers, subject to strict laws, and often went to great lengths to define who was of Aboriginal origin and thus subject to these laws. There was no real enthusiasm for improving Aboriginal welfare—instead the emphasis remained on what Aborigines could *not* do, with scarcely any willingness to allow Aborigines themselves to determine their future.

By 1937 there were some signs of change. Several Aboriginal and white groups wanted to end the concentration on protection. They sought instead the introduction of more positive policies. One instance of a more enlightened view came in the founding of Ernabella Mission, on the traditional land of the Pitjantjatjara people in north-western South Australia. Sponsored by Dr Charles Duguid and the Presbyterian Church, and supported by the South Australian government, it was established with much greater respect for Aboriginal language and culture, and sought to advance the employment, health and integrity of the local groups.

At the same time anthropological work in Australia was beginning to provide a different view of Aboriginal society from the usual white view. It suggested that traditional society was much more complex than normally believed—and not to be dismissed as 'primitive'. Traditional society had been well ordered and stable, with strong bonds between its members and sturdy practices

Aboriginal domestic trainees at Cootamundra Home, operated by the New South Wales Aboriginal Protection Board, about 1930

of sharing and religious observance. In its place a sorry picture had emerged—Aborigines had not been protected by policies of protection, and much of their traditional life had been broken down. The great majority of traditional groups had been effectively destroyed, especially in Victoria and Tasmania. They had had neither the time nor the opportunity to adjust meaningfully and with dignity to the European invasion. Members of Aboriginal groups that had managed to survive in some form were often forced to live in depressed physical circumstances and without the psychological comfort found in traditional life. Above all, nothing had compensated Aborigines for the loss of the land.

In the period just before the Second World War some effort was made to revise former policies. A conference of state and federal ministers in Canberra in 1937 agreed that 'the destiny of the natives of Aboriginal origin, but not of the full-blood, lies in their ultimate absorption by the people of the Commonwealth'. Whites, again claiming to decide what was best for Aborigines, were trying to bring about the disappearance of people with Aboriginal blood. The method favoured was to assimilate them into white society. Full-blood Aborigines were meanwhile to be supervised on pastoral stations and reserves, while those living in the large reserves such as Arnhem Land could preserve their traditional way of life, at least for the time being.

The Situation in the late 1930s

By 1939 the idea of eventual assimilation of all Aboriginal people into the white population was gaining ground. In that year the federal government spoke of eventual citizenship. Yet officially protection remained in force, and the restrictive laws continued to produce injustice and resentment. Aborigines, for example, were usually not allowed to travel freely within the states, while on the reserves their private lives were subject to many restrictions: their personal letters could be interfered with; they had to seek permission to marry; and children, especially part-Aboriginal children, could be removed from their parents. White officials controlled their employment opportunities and their personal financial affairs. In addition, especially in the northern pastoral industry, Aborigines would often be paid very little money or only their rations. In matters such as the right to vote,

Aborigines were again greatly disadvantaged.

As well as these humiliating conditions, the reduced numbers of the population indicated the Aborigines' misfortunes after the white invasion of the country. Although no accurate census figures for Aborigines were available, their population in 1938 was about 70 000. The great majority of them lived in northern Australia. Mission stations and government reserves were the homes of many: among these were Moore River in Western Australia, Lake Tyers in eastern Victoria, Point Pearce and Point Macleay in South Australia, Cherbourg and Palm Island in Queensland, and a large number of reserves in New South Wales such as at Cumeroogunga (in the Riverina) and Brewarrina. But none of the reserves or mission land was owned by the Aborigines themselves. The intention was to give some protection to Aborigines but at the same time keep them separate from white society.

Not surprisingly, many Aborigines were resentful at what had occurred under white settlement. They resisted against white policies. Resentment became more obvious at the 150th anniversary of white settlement in Australia. Aborigines in New South Wales, after protesting for years about the restrictive policies, decided through their Aborigines' Progressive Association to commemorate Australia Day, 26 January 1938, as a day of mourning. The Association wanted to protest 'on the anniversary of the white man's seizure of our country against the callous treatment of our people during the past 150 years'. The Association appealed for new laws for the education and care of Aborigines, and sought a policy which would raise Aborigines to full citizenship and civil equality with whites.

Mary Gilmore, the noted white writer and poet, supported the call. She declared that as a child she had seen Aborigines massacred in hundreds. They had been lying dead around poisoned waterholes, and she had seen hunting parties gather. Dogs had been imported from Europe because they were more savage. She had seen children dead in the grass, and scalps of Aborigines paid for as if they were dingoes.[10]

The Aborigines' Progressive Association put forward its own claims by speaking to whites:

You are the new Australians, but we are the old Australians. You came here only recently, and you took our land from us by force. You have almost exterminated our people, but there are enough of us remaining to expose the humbug of your claim, as white Australians, to be a civilized, progressive, kindly and humane nation . . . We do not wish to be regarded with sentimental sympathy, or to be 'preserved,' like koala bears, as exhibits; but we do ask for your real sympathy, and understanding . . .

We ask you to teach our people to live in the modern age as modern citizens. Our people are good and quick in assimilating knowledge. Why do you deliberately keep us backward? Is it merely to give yourselves the pleasure of feeling superior? Give our children the same chances as your own, and they will do as well as white children. We ask you to be proud of the Australian Aborigines and not to be misled any longer by the superstition that we are a naturally backward and low race. This is a scientific lie, which has helped to push our people down and down into the mire.

At worst, we are no more dirty, lazy, stupid, criminal or immoral, than white people. Also, your slanders against our race are moral lies, told to throw all the blame for our troubles on to us. You, who originally conquered us by guns against our spears, now rely on superiority of numbers to support your false claims of moral and intellectual superiority.[11]

In these words the Aboriginal view of white settlement and policies was put forward, forcibly and with much feeling, just before the problems of the Second World War emerged.

1 Beaglehole, J.C. (ed.) *The Journals of Captain James Cook* . . . Cambridge University Press, Cambridge, 1955, quoted in Clark, C.M.H. *A History of Australia*, Melbourne University Press, Melbourne, 1962, p. 51.
2 Kittle, S. *Concise History of the Colony and Natives of New South Wales*, Edinburgh, 1814, p. 180.
3 Tatz, C.M. *Four Kinds of Dominion*, Armidale, 1972, p. 16.
4 Breton, Lt. *Excursions in New South Wales, Western Australia, and Van Diemen's Land* . . . London, 1833, pp. 196, 200.
5 Curr, E.M. *The Australian Race*, Government Printer, Melbourne, 1886, vol. 1, p. 209.
6 *Illustrated Melbourne Post*, 13 August 1868.
7 Quotations from Roth's Report are in Bennett, M.M. *The Australian Aboriginal as a Human Being*, London, 1930, pp. 63–67.
8 *South Australian Register*, 24 November 1902.
9 Duguid, C. *No Dying Race*, Rigby, Adelaide, 1963, p. 138.
10 *Sydney Morning Herald*, 4 March 1938.
11 *The Argus* (Melbourne), 13 January 1938.

A NEW DEAL FOR ABORIGINAL PEOPLE?

5

By 1939, when the Second World War began, Aborigines had clearly suffered disastrously from white occupation of Australia. Cities, towns and fenced properties had been marked out on Aboriginal land, and much of Aboriginal traditional society had been destroyed. The destruction continued after 1939. New terms such as advancement, integration and land rights, however, at length began to be heard, as Aborigines increased their resistance to white domination. The pressure strengthened to confront whites with what had happened in the past and bring about change.

Aborigines and Policies after 1945

The Second World War had a strong impact on Aborigines. While it delayed or cancelled new government policies towards them, it gave Aborigines greater contact with whites, especially at army depots and other places where jobs were available. As in the First World War, some Aborigines enlisted and played a direct part in the war effort. Aborigines also moved increasingly to towns and cities, where they found work and made others more conscious of Aboriginal affairs. The Aboriginal population was also increasing, and the older European idea that the race would die out was now clearly proved wrong.

The Aboriginal migration to urban areas continued after war's end. Yet restrictive laws survived from pre-war days, and gaining exemption from them was difficult and undignified. On reserves, conditions remained depressed. Aborigines were forced to live in circumstances far worse than those of whites. In 1945 in north-western New South Wales, for example, where natural food and

provisions were sometimes unobtainable, a typical day's
diet on one government reserve was:

Breakfast: Tea and damper. Dinner: Bread and jam,
sometimes soup. Supper: Meat and bread or damper, tea.
On the river bank near the same station: Tea and damper for
every meal; occasionally saveloys for supper.

The situation was described further:

The children . . . suffer from impetigo (skin disease), running
noses, susceptibility to colds, and general malnutrition . . .[1]

Governments, now turning to a policy of assimilation
of Aborigines, had difficulty in introducing the policy.
Restrictive laws had to be removed before Aborigines
could be legally, socially and economically equal to
whites. Much greater attention had to be paid to Aboriginal welfare. Above all, there had to be a change in
white attitudes towards Aborigines.

Attempts were made to establish closer federal and
state cooperation in Aboriginal affairs. A conference in
1948 was a beginning, and policy discussions continued
at other meetings. In 1951 agreement was reached on the
general principle of assimilation of Aborigines and part-
Aborigines. All were 'expected eventually to attain the
same manner of living as other Australians, and to live
as members of a single Australian community'. Welfare
services and payments were also introduced or increased,
and mission stations were given more assistance or were
taken over by governments. In 1965 the assimilation policy was restated, so that it became one of integration. The
emphasis moved from the suppression of Aboriginal culture and the disintegration of the race towards the
Aborigines' right to retain their culture and identity within the Australian community.

But the restrictive laws at the heart of the protection
policy were difficult to remove. Until well into the 1960s
in each Australian state, control over Aboriginal lives—
over travel, employment, possessions, marriage and
other personal matters—remained oppressive. Only after
long campaigns was much progress achieved and legal
discrimination against Aborigines lessened. Equal pay for
Aborigines was one of the first achievements. Laws
against Aboriginal drinking of alcoholic liquor were

*A cottage—exterior and
interior—on a government
Aboriginal reserve, 1956*

gradually relaxed. Aborigines were allowed to travel or marry without special government approval. Voting rights were given. In 1966 the South Australian government granted Aborigines the right to control Aboriginal reserves, and passed a law to prohibit acts of discrimination against any racial group. In 1967 an important Commonwealth referendum decision gave the federal government greater power to make laws relating to Aborigines and decided Aborigines should be counted in future censuses.

The federal government, however, proved reluctant to legislate about Aboriginal affairs. Some states stubbornly retained restrictive laws. Queensland Acts in 1965 and 1971 ensured that Aborigines on reserves remained subject to regulations restricting freedom of expression and decision making. Aborigines could not have ownership of the reserves, and access to the reserves was restricted. One critic described these restrictions as 'an intolerable invasion of the rights of free movement and freedom of speech and opinion'. Aborigines expressed their opposition to such laws through the Federal Council for the Advancement of Aborigines, a body which from 1964 also represented Torres Strait Islanders. Already—in 1965—attention had been drawn to other injustices. Led by Charles Perkins (who was to become the first Aboriginal university graduate) and travelling by bus, university students went on a 'freedom ride' through towns in northern New South Wales, drawing attention to con-

Aborigines crossing Apsley Strait in canoes to vote at Bathurst Island, Northern Territory

ditions which Aborigines had to endure there. Their ride succeeded in bringing national publicity to practices of discrimination against Aborigines. Charles Perkins later recalled what happened in one town:

It was sensational, the effect the demonstration had upon people . . . All the hatred and confused thinking about race boiled to the surface and it was like a volcano exploding. For the first time in their lives people were running around and arguing these points with each other about a very tricky racial situation that was a complete embarrassment to them all. The Aborigines had been suppressed for so long.[2]

Land Rights

In the 1960s, as progress came on other matters, there was a stronger focus on Aboriginal land rights. In traditional society land was central to people's lives, binding Aborigines in a special, spiritual relationship to certain areas. This relationship had been interrupted by European occupation, and no compensation had been made. To Aborigines the issue of land rights involved restoring what was rightfully theirs, though many whites saw it as an attempt to get something for nothing. The issue also challenged the assimilation ideal, for land rights would allow Aborigines to live separately.

The land rights question brought hard-fought campaigns. In one of the best-known, a large group of Aborigines, mostly of Gurindji ancestry, left their camp at Wave Hill station in the Northern Territory in 1966. They had grievances—low pay, poor food and long hours of work—against the British company holding the pastoral lease. But the Gurindjis were fired most of all by a desire to have their own land, and moved to a new camp at Daguradu (Wattie Creek), one of their sacred sites. Their leader Vincent Lingiari said they had decided 'to cease to live like dogs'. In 1967 they laid claim to an area of about 1 300 square kilometres for their own cattle station within the lease. They petitioned the Australian governor-general for a return of their land. The federal government, responsible for the Northern Territory, rejected the request, favouring a new Aboriginal town centre at Wave Hill. The issue smouldered. The Gurindjis, supported by southerners, including whites, kept up their demand for land. Some progress came in

1972, when the government agreed that Aborigines could hold leases and the pastoral company agreed to surrender part of their lease. Yet no rights to own the land were granted.

The land rights struggle also involved mining companies. In 1963 Aborigines at Yirrkala, in north-eastern Arnhem Land, objected to a lease of part of their land to a Swiss company for bauxite mining. The Yirrkala sent a bark petition to the federal parliament, claiming the land to be part of their own country and not something they had agreed to grant away. Despite rejections of their claim, the struggle went on. In 1971 the Yirrkala appealed to the Northern Territory Supreme Court, which declared there had been no 'civilised' Aboriginal government owning the land when it was first explored and claimed by whites.

To Aborigines and an increasing number of whites, this and other denials of Aboriginal land rights were wrong. The Yirrkala people protested against the court's decision, petitioning the prime minister. Though the case aroused international discussion, mining went ahead and

Members of an Aboriginal tent embasssy in Adelaide talking to the Aboriginal Senator Neville Bonner, September 1972. Note the Aboriginal flag

the town of Nhulunbuy grew, with Aborigines still claiming the land and mining royalties. Aborigines were succeeding in making land rights a major political issue. Their campaign soon took a novel form. Aboriginal encampments, or 'embassies', appeared in cities. In Canberra, on Australia Day, 1972, Aborigines set up a tent embassy in front of Parliament House. Staffed at various times by Aborigines from across Australia, the embassy members demanded crown and reserve land, as well as significant monetary compensation for land taken in the past. Clearly not all Aborigines were content with the limited land rights already granted in some states. They felt the federal government must recognise the Aborigines' right to their traditional land—land which they had never granted away and in fact could not do so. The Aboriginal leader Bobbi Sykes made the position clear:

The Embassy symbolized that blacks had been pushed as far back as blacks are going to be pushed . . . First and foremost it symbolized the land rights struggle. But beyond that, it said to white Australia, 'You've kicked us down for the last time.' In all areas. In education, in health, in police victimization, in locking people up en masse—in all these things. It said that blacks were now going to get up and fight back on any or all these issues.[3]

The election of a federal Labor government in 1972 encouraged Aborigines, though there was caution about the new National Aboriginal Consultative Committee and the setting up of a land rights commission, headed by Mr Justice Woodward, in 1973–74. Recommendations in the Woodward reports guided government actions, leading to the Aboriginal Land Rights (Northern Territory) Act in 1976. This Act at last entitled Aborigines in the Northern Territory to own traditional land and claim vacant Crown land under certain conditions. The Act became an example for governments elsewhere.

Land rights matters advanced unevenly. In 1974 there was finally some satisfaction over the Gurindji claims, when land was divided and the Gurindjis received the documents for a new pastoral lease. In Victoria Aborigines had received title to the reserves at Framlingham and Lake Tyers in 1970. In South Australia, though the Aboriginal Lands Trust had been set up in 1966, it was difficult to reach agreement about land grants in the north-west of the state. Some whites were anxious to

Pitjantjatjara people demonstrating for land rights, Adelaide 1980

preserve mineral rights there, whereas Aborigines wanted unrestricted title. In 1980 the Pitjantjatjara people brought the issue to a head by travelling to Adelaide in buses and camping on a city racecourse. Their council and the South Australian government finally reached a compromise about how any mining could be carried out and how royalties should be shared. Subject to the special conditions, the numerous Pitjantjatjara people and their neighbours were given freehold title in 1981 to a very large area, enabling the Pitjantjatjara Council to proceed with efforts to administer the area as an Aboriginal homeland. In 1984 the Maralinga lands to the south were also granted to Aboriginal owners by the South Australian government. Northwards, in the Northern Territory, difficulties occurred over land rights concerning Uluru (Ayers Rock) and surrounding land. The matter was finally resolved in 1985: the national park land was granted to the Mutitjulu people, who in turn granted a lease to federal authorities to allow tourist access to continue.

Whites' anxiety to have access to land, especially for mining purposes, was a major hurdle in land rights arrangements. Federal and state disagreements made things worse. In Queensland in the 1970s the right to mine for bauxite roused arguments between governments about the Aurukun and Mornington Island Aboriginal settlements. The arguments continued in the 1980s, with the Queensland government keeping ultimate control, especially over mining, in the reserves. At Noonkanbah, in the Kimberley district of Western Australia, Aborigines objected again to a mining lease over Aboriginal station land. The Western Australian government determined that exploration should go ahead, even using police in 1980 to escort an oil rig into the Noonkanbah land. In the

Noonkanbah demonstration, Western Australia, 1981

Northern Territory, Aboriginal land councils became engaged in long negotiations about rights to extract uranium, oil and gas on traditional Aboriginal land. In some states slow progress marred land transfers to Aboriginal Land Trusts. Slow progress, too, marred government willingness to grant monetary compensation to Aborigines for past land losses. In Tasmania descendants of the original Aborigines—thought to have died out but who had left survivors from their intermarriage with Europeans—recognised themselves as Aboriginal people. The Tasmanian government, however, resisted their efforts in the early 1980s to gain land rights.

By the 1980s the Aboriginal campaign for land had achieved a measure of success. In many cases former mission land and reserves had passed to Aboriginal control and ownership, a process begun by the South Australian Aboriginal Lands Trust legislation in 1966. The Northern Territory Act of 1976, allowing land rights, was another milestone. The setting up of land councils in the Northern Territory and New South Wales enabled Aborigines to own land there. But much of the land granted to Aborigines in Australia was in remote central and northern areas. At the end of the 1980s Tasmanian Aborigines still held no land, and little land was held in Victoria and New South Wales. Strong opposition to Aboriginal land rights came from mining and rural interests, hindering the full exercise and extension of Aboriginal land ownership. Nor did whites easily accept that the descendants of Aborigines who had lost land in the past should receive land grants in modern times as compensation. Land rights remained a stubborn, but very live, issue.

The Homelands or Outstation Movement

In recent decades some Aborigines have come to prefer living in communities on traditional land away from towns and larger settlements. In the 1970s a steady flow of people moved from townships and reserves to outstations or homeland centres, especially in northern and central Australia. The pressures and stress in larger settlements encouraged this movement, which brought hundreds of outstations into existence. Aborigines thus gained greater control over their own affairs, though the homeland settlements have often maintained contact with larger centres such as Oenpelli, Aurukun and Ernabella. Government health and educational services have been extended to these settlements. The essential feature has been the wish of small groups of Aborigines, usually with kinship ties between individual members, to live as independently as possible. As with land rights generally, the movement to new settlements came not from a demand to seize property but from a desire to restore a close relationship with the land. This desire had also been shown in the long, and finally successful, campaign to make the British government agree to clear contaminated soil from the former atomic testing site on the Maralinga lands in South Australia.

The Mabo Judgment and Native Title

The Mabo judgment, delivered by the High Court of Australia in 1992, turned the whole question of land rights in a new direction and became a landmark in Aboriginal affairs. The Mabo case began in 1982, when Eddie Mabo and other residents of Mer (Murray Island) in the Torres Strait, all members of the Meriam people, sought a court declaration of their land rights. They argued that because unbroken generations of their people had lived on Mer and the adjacent islands, they were the customary owners and held a traditional 'native title' over the islands and nearby seas, a title existing before British settlement in

Eddie Mabo, of Murray Island, whose name has been given to the High Court judgment of 1992, the year of his death

Australia and not granted by any government. The Queensland government, opposing that claim, passed a law in 1985 which confirmed its opinion that the traditional title had been extinguished. The High Court, however, ruled that the Queensland law clashed with the federal Racial Discrimination Act of 1976. The High Court finally gave its Mabo decision on 3 June 1992 (some months after Eddie Mabo's death). It declared that no laws had deprived the Meriam people of their continuing native title under common law—'the Meriam people are entitled as against the whole world to possession, occupation, use and enjoyment of the lands of the Murray Islands'. The judgment overturned the old idea that when the British occupied Australia the land was practically unoccupied and belonged to no-one, the idea expressed in the Latin phrase *terra nullius*, 'no-one's land'. The judgment stated that the Aboriginal people had not been nomads, but a people with a strong traditional relationship to their land and with ties of ownership to it.

The Mabo judgment suggested that the decision could apply elsewhere in Australia. Native title could survive where Aborigines had maintained their relationship to the land and where governments had not extinguished native title by special laws or grants of freehold titles and leases. Much land, however, in Australia's settled districts, including town, city and farming land, had already been secured under freehold (the title giving exclusive ownership) or lease (the title applying where government land was leased for a period). On this kind of property, the High Court said, native title had been extinguished and Aborigines could not claim it. The widespread fears of non-Aborigines that privately-owned land could be taken away were thus mistaken, and it was likely that successful Aboriginal claims would mostly succeed only for remote and undeveloped government land. The court also said that Aborigines would not receive direct compensation for land lost in the past, nor could they have sovereignty over any part of Australia.

The fears of non-Aboriginal groups, such as mining companies, pastoralists and governments, led to confusion and resentment after the Mabo decision, even though it was clear that Aboriginal groups would find it difficult to prove that they had maintained their traditional connection to an area of land. Questions arose—if a grant of pasturage rights had not extinguished native title, could Aborigines claim a pastoral lease over the land granted? Would native title harm the activities of mining companies? Several state governments were alarmed. To clarify the situation further and set down proper procedures, the federal government introduced native title legislation, resulting in the Native Title Act of December 1993. Tribunals and court hearings were provided for, to help decide native title questions, and a National Native Title Tribunal, to deal with applications and compensation matters, was established in Perth. The Native Title Act also provided for a national land fund—the National Aboriginal and Torres Strait Islander Land Fund—which began on 1 July 1994. The idea was that land could be bought for the large number of dispossessed Aborigines, often in towns and cities, who no longer had direct links to their traditional land and thus did not benefit from the Mabo decision.

The Mabo judgment and the Native Title Act did not solve everyone's land questions. Some state governments remained unhappy about the possible impact on mining and pastoralism. Another consequence of the Mabo judgment and the Native Title Act was a stream of native title claims. It was feared that these claims, covering large areas of land, might test the tolerance of non-Aborigines towards measures helping Aborigines. This fear came when the process of reconciliation between Aborigines and non-Aborigines was being given a fresh start.

Health and Population

The health of Aborigines declined quickly after white settlement began. Besides the impact of diseases caught from Europeans, the health of Aborigines was affected by the loss of land. This loss reduced their opportunities for normal hunting and gathering, in turn reducing their food supply and diet balance. The result was often malnutrition or even starvation. Rations supplied at white mission stations and reserves proved an inadequate substitute for the traditional foods. The loss of land also robbed Aborigines of their self-confidence and spirit, again harming their personal health.

Aboriginal ill health has remained a serious problem. Governments have been criticised for inadequate health programs because the diseases affecting Aborigines have usually been preventable and curable. Surveys have exposed the health problems. Infant mortality has always been, and is still, higher among Aborigines than among whites—in 1978, for example, deaths among Aboriginal infants in the Northern Territory were five times higher than among white children. Improving health services have caused this rate to decline, but infant mortality among Aborigines nationally is still three times the rate among non-Aborigines. Ear, nose, throat and respiratory infections have been common among Aboriginal children, who have also been more likely to suffer from gastroenteritis, skin complaints, tooth decay and eye infections. Trachoma, an eye infection that can lead to blindness, has been widespread, particularly among Aboriginal people in inland areas. Among older Aborigines leprosy and tuberculosis have also been serious diseases; for many years Australia had one of the highest rates of leprosy in the world. A potent cause of poor health has been poor living conditions: inadequate water supplies and sewerage, overcrowded housing and unhealthy diet have each contributed to this problem. In 1991 there were 251 Aboriginal communities without an electricity supply.

While the federal government has aimed to raise the level of Aboriginal health to the national standard, in recent years more Aborigines have suffered illnesses familar among whites, such as heart disease, blood pressure problems and diabetes. Excessive consumption of alcohol has also affected Aboriginal health and community stability. Aborigines have become concerned about improving health education and the facilities for treatment. But the disruption to Aboriginal health since 1788 has left a bitter legacy. Despite increased government spending, Aboriginal mortality rates have remained significantly higher than among whites: the 1991 census showed the life expectancy for Aboriginal and Torres Strait Islander males to be 57 years, compared to 74 years for all males generally; for women, 65 years, compared with 80 years.

Although life expectancy is lower, the census total of the Aboriginal population has been steadily increasing. One factor has been the higher Aboriginal birth rate since 1980; another has been the increasing readiness of people to class themselves as Aborigines and to be included in the census. The total population of Aborigines and Torres Strait Islanders in the 1971 census was 115 953; in 1986 it was 227 645; and in 1991 it was 265 458. (Of the 1991 total, 238 575 were Aborigines and 26 883 were Torres Strait Islanders.) In 1991 more than half of the Aboriginal and Islander people lived in New South Wales and Queensland. Two-thirds of the Aboriginal population lived in urban areas, while only in the Northern Territory was the population strongly rural. Sydney, with 22 905 Aboriginal people, was the region with the highest population in 1991. The censuses of 1971 and 1991 showed the population growth of Aborigines and Torres Strait Islanders in each state:

	1971	1991
Queensland	31 922	70 127
New South Wales	23 873	70 019
Western Australia	22 181	41 778
Northern Territory	23 381	39 915
South Australia	7 299	16 231
Victoria	6 371	16 735
Tasmania	671	8 884
Australian Capital Territory	255	1 775
TOTAL	**115 953**	**265 458**

The Aboriginal and Islander population was also shown to be much more youthful (with a median age of 19 in 1991) than the total Australian population (median age 32).

Education and Languages

In the past, Aborigines have often had limited opportunities to attend schools and universities. Government education schemes have also usually assumed that only European culture and skills should be taught to Aborigines. From 1970, however, the Aboriginal Secondary Grants Scheme began to provide assistance for secondary education, and assistance also became available for higher training. The teaching of Aboriginal languages and culture was introduced more readily in Aboriginal communities. Bilingual education has thus become available in remote areas where Aboriginal schools have been established. In these schools pride in Aboriginal identity has been

Mandawuy Yunupingu, lead singer of Yothu Yindi, a highly successful Aboriginal band

emphasised, instead of the older emphasis in schools on replacing Aboriginal culture with that of Europeans. But some statistics relating to Aborigines and schooling have caused concern. In 1988 only 17% of Aboriginal students remained to the senior level of secondary school, compared with 57% of other students, and in 1991 5% of Aborigines aged over fourteen had never attended school.

In fostering Aboriginal languages schools have begun to play an important role, though many languages have already died out, along with the Aboriginal groups speaking them. About a hundred languages survive in some form, but few are widely used and more may disappear. In the past the teaching of English, as part of the assimilation policy, was another reason for the decline of the traditional languages. Modern methods of communication, however, have been helping to arrest the decline. Imparja, an Aboriginal-owned commercial satellite television service, began operating from Alice Springs in 1988. Though not planned as a solely Aboriginal service, Imparja included in its aims the development of Aboriginal secondary school programs and the promotion of Aboriginal languages.

Housing

In the matter of housing, conditions for Aborigines have been far below the general Australian standard for many decades. Aborigines have commonly been forced to live in makeshift accommodation on the fringe of towns or at station camps. Housing on Aboriginal reserves has often been poor. An observer described a typical example, near Wilcannia in New South Wales in 1965:

A dusty track leads you . . . into a compound of 14 identical houses, built barracks-like, in two parallel rows . . . This desert ghetto is the government Aboriginal reserve where 80 people endure a primitive existence without electricity, sinks or baths. Only three houses have stoves . . . The Aboriginal Welfare Board built this compound and owns the houses, which many of its tenants find most useful for the firewood they provide.[4]

Beyond this reserve conditions were no better. In a shanty town nearby there were more than forty shacks made of bags and tin, with no water, electricity, stoves or baths. Elsewhere things were often as bad: in 1971 a professor of child health described settlement houses near

Alice Springs as 'aluminium dog kennels with concrete floors ... up to 20 degrees(F) hotter in summer and 20 degrees(F) colder in winter than the rubbish-heap humpy. Most contain no furniture, fireplace or running water'.[5] In 1976 a survey in New South Wales showed that half of the state's Aboriginal people lived in inferior housing, which contributed to poor health. In 1977 the federal minister for Aboriginal affairs recognised that housing was frequently of poor quality and design, and spoke of 'the appalling housing situation of so many Aboriginal families'.

Houses at a government Aboriginal reserve, 1965

At the end of the 1980s Aboriginal housing remained at a lower standard than that enjoyed by whites. One problem was the shortage of houses; another was the fact that many Aborigines could not afford to buy them. The situation was one in which poor housing, poor health and a lack of educational opportunities were all intermingled. Government schemes have concentrated on providing funds for house purchase, house rental and hostel accommodation. Much remains to be done—it was estimated in 1989 that one-third of all Aboriginal families had inadequate housing and lacked essential services such as suitable drinking water, electricity supply, waste and sewerage disposal, and sealed roads. Increasing amounts are now being allocated to housing loans, but Aborigines still face a serious shortage of housing, together with overcrowding in many existing houses.

Legal Matters

The history of contact between Aborigines and Europeans in Australia has involved much legal questioning and procedure. Aboriginal law, a binding force in traditional society, was not recognised by early European colonists, who declared that Aborigines must observe the Europeans' law and be responsible in the law courts for any violations of it. Aboriginal law, and the Aboriginal right to the land, was not taken into account in these courts.

In modern times some court hearings have been concerned with Aboriginal land rights. But far more often they have involved actions against Aborigines for various offences. There has also been evidence of strained relations between Aborigines and the police. This has continued the pattern in colonial times, but it has become clear that the pattern should be broken. Statistics have revealed that Aborigines in the modern period have been charged, convicted and imprisoned for offences (chiefly minor ones) at a much higher rate than the rest of the population. The matter has become complex and disturbing, raising many

Michael (Mick) Dodson, Victoria's first Aboriginal lawyer

questions about the reasons for the high rate, about how justice is administered, about the appropriateness of punishments, and so on. A grim feature has been the number of deaths among Aborigines held in custody, which prompted the federal government in 1987 to order a special inquiry into the circumstances of these deaths. The result was the Royal Commission into Aboriginal Deaths in Custody. In investigating ninety-nine deaths, the commission examined a range of matters in detail. In its final report in 1991 it made 339 recommendations. The commission found that the disturbing rate of deaths in custody had deep-seated causes, linked to the disdavantaged and unequal position of Aborigines in Australian society. Better relations between white and black people could only come when the rights, culture and traditions of Aboriginal people were recognised, and when there was a 'complete rejection of concepts of superiority and inferiority'. Reconciliation and self-determination, the commission reported, were essential ingredients of any improvement in Aboriginal affairs.

A Treaty and Reconciliation

The unhappy contact between Aborigines and whites in Australia since 1788 has left a sense of injustice among the Aboriginal people. In discussions about overcoming this problem, a remedy has been suggested: what is needed is not just another law but an end to arguing and an acceptance of normal relations. ('Makarrata' is an Aboriginal term for this idea.) To bring this about, a treaty between Aboriginal and white Australians has been proposed—a treaty within Australia between Australians. By itself a treaty may not solve problems, but it may express agreement about the rights and proper position of Aborigines in Australian society.

Progress towards such a treaty has been uncertain, and the idea itself has been opposed. An Aboriginal opinion in 1980 was that compensation for losses of land and culture would also be needed, and this should be paid in kind and in cash. An example has been set in other countries, which have agreed on terms for compensating their native peoples for land loss. The Australian prime minister in the late 1980s supported the treaty idea. Some Aboriginal leaders have stated that a treaty should be based on fixed principles, which were defined in a statement to the prime

minister at Barunga in the Northern Territory in June 1988. The principles included Aboriginal control over ancestral lands, self-determination, compensation for lost land, protection for sacred sites and objects, and respect for and promotion of Aboriginal identity and language.

Political support after 1988 for such a treaty was hesitant. Instead of a treaty, the suggestion of a 'compact' or some form of 'reconciliation' became more attractive. The federal parliament took an important step in 1991 by agreeing to form the Council for Aboriginal Reconciliation. The council,

A Pitjantjatjara group at Everard Park station, South Australia, in 1972. They told the photographer they wanted land so they could compete economically with whites and preserve the lands of the Dreaming

comprising twenty-five prominent Australians—Aboriginal and non-Aboriginal—and with Mr Pat Dodson as chairman, was given the task of working towards reconciliation between Aborigines and other Australians through various measures before the year 2001. The framework of reconciliation could be expressed in a 'document of reconciliation'. The council put forward a vision: 'A united Australia which respects this land of ours; values the Aboriginal and Torres Strait Islander heritage; and provides justice and equity for all'. In 1995 the council made further proposals for social justice for Aborigines, including recognition of the Aboriginal flag and some political representation for Aborigines.

Aboriginal Organisations and Responsibility—ATSIC

After the 1967 referendum gave it greater power in Aboriginal affairs, the federal government set up the Council for Aboriginal Affairs as an advisory body. From 1972 the Department of Aboriginal Affairs began to administer matters relating to Aborigines and Torres Strait Islanders. Other federal bodies, such as the Australian Institute of Aboriginal Studies (1964) and the Aboriginal Development Commission (1980), were established for special tasks.

Aboriginal people themselves now play a much greater role in shaping policies. An emphasis on self-determination and autonomy for local communities has emerged. The founding of Aboriginal land councils has been one example. Another has been the formation of ATSIC—the Aboriginal and Torres Strait Islander Commission, now the chief policy-maker and administrator in Aboriginal affairs. ATSIC was set up in March 1990, taking over responsibilities from the federal Department of Aboriginal Affairs and the Aboriginal Development Commission. ATSIC is a unique body, allowing Aborigines and Torres Strait Islanders to elect representatives to thirty-five regional councils. The regional councils, which play a key role in ATSIC's work, appoint seventeen commissioners to ATSIC's council; two more members are appointed by the federal minister. The federal government has delegated power to it, and ATSIC decides programs and controls spending, in keeping with the principle of self-determination. Increasingly, grants are made to local organisations for housing, employment, water and electricity supplies, land purchases, development of businesses and other services. But for a number of Aborigines, ATSIC is not the ideal; it represents another bureaucratic body involved in Aboriginal affairs. Some kind of regional authority, they claim, would be a more efficient administrative body in many areas.

Employment and Achievement

Aboriginal people have often been handicapped by few available jobs, low wages and a lack of training. The system of Aborigines receiving lower than the award wages, which was frequently found in the pastoral industry, has been overturned. The lack of suitable training and of jobs, however, has survived. Unemployment among Aborigines has remained much higher than the rate for non-Aborigines. To a large extent this has been due to a

Cathy Freeman, a brilliant sprinter, carrying the Aboriginal flag

shortage of work in small towns and remote areas. To meet this problem, Aboriginal communities have started to define the kind of employment needed. ATSIC's biggest commitment now is to the Community Development Employment Projects (CDEP) scheme. This scheme, originating in 1976, enables Aborigines and Torres Strait Islanders to work on a part-time basis, instead of receiving unemployment benefits, on projects to improve their communities. By 1995 about 25 000 people were working under this scheme. Many projects, such as the development of cattle stations, have been successfully undertaken.

Fortunately the old white belief that Aborigines were incapable of reaching the same standards as whites has been largely broken down. High-level Aboriginal graduates from universities, skilled Aboriginal administrators, artisans and others in a variety of trades and professions— all have revealed the ability of the Aboriginal people to succeed in a wide range of fields. Aborigines have distinguished themselves in many activities and positions formerly associated only with whites. They have made their mark in sport at both national and international levels. In the arts, such as literature, painting and the dramatic arts, they have achieved at a very high level. One Aborigine, Sir Douglas Nicholls, an outstanding Victorian sportsman and campaigner for Aboriginal advancement, rose to become governor of South Australia in 1976. Aboriginal people have proved that they are not inferior in ability or attainments.

Oodgeroo Noonuccal, known for much of her life as Kath Walker and highly regarded as a writer and worker for Aboriginal advancement

Identity

Much of the history of contact between whites and Aborigines in Australia has been about identity. Whites have tried, in one way or another, to suppress Aboriginal identity; in resisting, Aborigines have not only defended their identity but have sought more recently to assert it. Their willingness to do so is reflected in the rising census total of those who identify themselves as Aborigines. Aborigines have come to show pride in their 'blackness'— pride in their race and its spirit. Tasmanian Aborigines in particular have had to assert their identity positively, as non-Aborigines believed that they had died out in the nineteenth century. The Tasmanians survived largely as Islander communities in Bass Strait, and numbered 8 884 in 1991.

This pride in identity has led to new ways of expressing it. Some have wanted to do so by discarding the term Aborigines, first used by Europeans, and adopting another title. (Kooris has been used in Victoria and New South Wales, Nungas in South Australia, Murris in Queensland and Nyoongahs in Western Australia.) Positive steps have been taken in other ways to encourage the sense of Aboriginal identity. Many younger Aborigines, especially in the cities, where a majority now live, have been outspoken in demanding an improvement in the status of their people, and there is now much more emphasis on social justice for Aborigines. An awareness of previous injustice and loss of identity has made this demand keener. One of the worst injustices in the past was the policy of white authorities taking Aboriginal children from their parents and placing them under the care of whites, believing that this would be a means of advancing their assimilation. Evidence of this practice is now becoming more widely known and is being made the subject of a special inquiry.

For many Aborigines, identity is still about their relationship to the land. It is symbolised by the Aboriginal flag—the top half black, representing the people; the bottom half red, representing the land; and a central golden disc representing the sun, the renewer of life. The flag has been flown since the 1960s, especially in land rights struggles. The flag is a symbol that possession of land—at the heart of traditional society and Aboriginal identity—remains a crucial issue. If control of their land can be achieved, several Aboriginal groups then want regional authority to be placed in their own hands. This would allow them to do things themselves, instead of having to deal through a government agency or ATSIC. For some groups this would be a valuable step towards their goal of self-rule, something which their ancestors once enjoyed but which had been torn away by European settlement.

1 Quoted in the *Sixteenth Annual Report of the Victorian Aboriginal Group*, Melbourne, 1945.
2 Perkins, C. *A Bastard Like Me*, Ure Smith, Sydney, 1975, p. 78.
3 Quoted in Gilbert, K.J. *Because a White Man'll Never Do It*, Angus and Robertson, Sydney, 1973, p. 29.
4 *Australian*, 4 January 1965.
5 *Sunday Mail* (Adelaide), 9 October 1971.

A Song of Hope

Look up, my people,
The dawn is breaking,
The world is waking
To a new bright day,
When none defame us,
No restriction tame us,
Nor colour shame us,
Nor sneer dismay.

Now brood no more
On the years behind you,
The hope assigned you
Shall the past replace,
When a juster justice
Grown wise and stronger
Points the bone no longer
At a darker race.

So long we waited
Bound and frustrated,
Till hate be hated
And caste deposed;
Now light shall guide us,
No goal denied us,
And all doors open
That long were closed.

See plain the promise,
Dark freedom-lover!
Night's nearly over,
And though long the
   climb,
New rights will greet us,
New mateship meet us,
And joy complete us
In our new Dream Time.

To our fathers' fathers
The pain, the sorrow;
To our children's children
The glad tomorrow.
Kath Walker.

A poem by Oodgeroo of the tribe Noonuccal (formerly Kath Walker), the noted Queensland Aboriginal poet, activist and educationist.

Reading List

The following reading list, divided into two groups according to the chapters in this book, is a selection of books that will be helpful in further study of Aboriginal life and experience in Australia. Most of these books are readily available.

Chapters 1–3 Traditional Society

Bell, D. *Daughters of the Dreaming*, McPhee Gribble/George Allen and Unwin, Melbourne, 1983.

Berndt, R.M. and C.H. *The World of the First Australians* (5th edn), Aboriginal Studies Press, Canberra, 1988.

Blainey, G. *Triumph of the Nomads: A History of Ancient Australia* (rev. edn), Macmillan, Melbourne, 1982.

Edwards, R. *Aboriginal Bark Canoes of the Murray Valley*, Rigby, Adelaide, 1972.

Edwards, R. *Australian Aboriginal Art: The Art of the Alligator Rivers Region, Northern Territory*, Australian Institute of Aboriginal Studies, Canberra, 1979.

Edwards, W.H. *An Introduction to Aboriginal Societies*, Social Science Press, Wentworth Falls, NSW, 1988.

Flood, Josephine *Archaeology of the Dreamtime* (rev. edn), Angus and Robertson, Sydney, 1995.

Flood, Josephine *The Riches of Ancient Australia* (rev. edn), University of Queensland Press, St Lucia, 1993.

Gale, Fay (ed.) *Woman's Role in Aboriginal Society* (3rd edn), Australian Institute of Aboriginal Studies, Canberra, 1978.

Haigh, C. and Goldstein, W. (eds) *The Aborigines of New South Wales*, NSW National Parks and Wildlife Service, Sydney, 1980.

Hardy, J. and Frost, A. (eds) *Studies from Terra Australis to Australia*, Australian Academy of the Humanities, Canberra, 1989.

Horton, D. (ed.) *The Encyclopaedia of Aboriginal Australia*, Aboriginal Studies Press, Canberra, 1994.

Isaacs, Jennifer *Aboriginality: Contemporary Aboriginal Paintings and Prints*, University of Queensland Press, St Lucia, 1989.

Isaacs, Jennifer (ed.) *Australian Dreaming: 40 000 Years of Aboriginal History*, Landsdowne Press, Sydney, 1980.

Maddock, K. *The Australian Aborigines: A Portrait of Their Society*, Penguin, Ringwood Victoria, 1982.

Mulvaney, D.J. *The Prehistory of Australia*, Penguin, Ringwood Victoria, 1975.

Mulvaney, D.J. and White, J.P. *Australians to 1788*, in *Australians: A Historical Library*, vol I, Fairfax, Syme and Weldon Associates, Sydney, 1987.

Presland, G. *The Land of the Kulin: Discovering the Lost Landscape and the First People of Port Phillip*, McPhee Gribble and Penguin, Melbourne, 1985.

Ryan, L. *The Aboriginal Tasmanians*, University of Queensland Press, Brisbane, 1981.

Sutton, P. (ed.) *Dreamings: The Art of Aboriginal Australia*, Viking, Melbourne, 1988.

Tindale, N.B. *The Aboriginal Tribes of Australia*, University of California Press, Berkeley, 1974.

Tunbridge, Dorothy *Flinders Ranges Dreaming*, Aboriginal Studies Press, Canberra, 1988.

White, J.P. and O'Connell, J.F. *A Prehistory of Australia, New Guinea and Sahul*, Academic Press, London, 1982.

Chapters 4–5 Conflict since 1788

Broome, R. *Aboriginal Australians* (2nd edn), Allen & Unwin, Sydney, 1994.

Butlin, N.G. *Our Original Aggression: Aboriginal Populations of South-eastern Australia, 1788–1850*, George Allen and Unwin, Sydney, 1983.

Charlesworth, M. *The Aboriginal Land Rights Movement* (2nd edn), Hodja Educational Resources, Melbourne, 1984.

Franklin, Margaret *Black and White Australians: An Inter-racial History 1788–1975*, Heinemann Educational, Melbourne, 1976.

Gale, Fay *Urban Aborigines*, ANU Press, Canberra, 1972.

Gilbert, A.D. and Inglis, K.S. (eds) *Australians: A Historical Library*, 10 vols, Fairfax, Syme and Weldon Associates, Sydney, 1987.

Gilbert, K. *Living Black: Blacks Talk to Kevin Gilbert*, Penguin, Ringwood Victoria, 1978.

Going Forward: Social Justice for the First Australians, A Submission to the Commonwealth Government, Council for Aboriginal Reconciliation, Canberra, 1995.

Jenkin, G.K. *Conquest of the Ngarrindjeri*, Rigby, Adelaide, 1979.

Lippmann, Lorna *Generations of Resistance: Mabo and Justice* (3rd edn), Longman Australia, Melbourne, 1994.

Mabo Papers, Parliamentary Research Service Subject Collection No. 1, Australian Government Publishing Service, Canberra, 1994.

Mattingley, Christobel (ed.) *Survival in Our Own Land: 'Aboriginal' Experiences in 'South Australia' Since 1836*, Wakefield Press, Adelaide, 1988.

Miller, J. *Koori: A Will to Win*, Angus and Robertson, Sydney, 1985.

Mulvaney, D.J. *Encounters in Place: Outsiders and Aboriginal Australians 1606–1985*, University of Queensland Press, St Lucia, 1989.

Perkins, C. *A Bastard Like Me*, Ure Smith, Sydney, 1975.

Reid, Gordon *A Picnic with the Natives: Aboriginal–European Relations in the Northern Territory to 1910*, Melbourne University Press, Melbourne, 1990.

Reynolds, H. *Frontier: Aborigines, Settlers and Land*, Allen & Unwin, Sydney, 1987.

Reynolds, H. *The Other Side of the Frontier: Aboriginal Resistance to the European Invasion of Australia*, Penguin, Ringwood Victoria, 1982.

Reynolds, H. *The Law of the Land*, Penguin, Ringwood Victoria, 1987.

Reynolds, H. *Dispossession: Black Australians and White Invaders*, Allen & Unwin, Sydney, 1989.

Reynolds, H. *Fate of a Free People*, Penguin, Ringwood Victoria, 1995.

Rowley, C.D. *Recovery: The Politics of Aboriginal Reform*, Penguin, Ringwood Victoria, 1986.

Rowley, C.D. *The Destruction of Aboriginal Society*, ANU Press, Canberra, 1970; *Outcasts in White Australia*, ANU Press, Canberra, 1971; *The Remote Aborigines*, ANU Press, Canberra, 1971.

Stanner, W.E.H. *White Man Got No Dreaming*, ANU Press, Canberra, 1979.

Walking Together: The First Steps, Report of the Council for Aboriginal Reconciliation to Federal Parliament 1991–94,

Australian Government Publishing Service, Canberra, 1994.

Willey, K. *When the Sky Fell Down: the Destruction of the Tribes of the Sydney Region 1788–1850s*, Collins, Sydney, 1979.

Yarwood, A.T. and Knowling, M.J. *Race Relations in Australia: a History*, Methuen, Sydney, 1982.

Young, Elspeth *Aborigines, Land and Society*, Longman Australia, Melbourne, 1993.

Research Exercises

Chapter 1

1 Look up a number of books, including school text
books, dealing with the general history of Australia.
How much attention and importance does each
writer give to the role of the Aboriginal people in
that history?
What conclusions can you draw about the writers

ARCHEOLOGY AT KOONALDA CAVE—1960

A . . . scientist, sitting one day this month at a stone table in the Nullarbor Plain's Koonalda
Cave, realised that an Aborigine had sat there at least 4,000 years ago making flint
implements.

The native 'tool factory' had just been uncovered by excavations . . .

The Koonalda Cave, which in parts extends for 1,600 ft (480 metres), has a ceiling up to
200 ft (60 metres) high.

Dr Alexander Gallus . . . described the discovery in Adelaide at the weekend.

'It was the greatest thrill of our lives suddenly to find this snapshot of interrupted prehistoric
activity,' he said.

'The products of this prehistoric workshop, 120 ft (35 metres) below the arid Nullarbor
Plain, the stone tools used to make them and the raw material (flint) lay all around, just as
the Aboriginal manufacturer had left them.

'In a hollow behind the work-bench lay a fist-size stone hammer of crystalline limestone.

'Apparently it had been used to flake strips from flint, held on a stone work-base, which still
lay on the bench.

'A pile of fresh flints, ready for working, lay beside the bench.

'Later excavations to about $4\frac{1}{2}$ ft ($1\frac{1}{2}$ metres) in the cave floor revealed stone implements,
made there up to about 12,000 years ago.

'This is the only spot in Australia where such an extraordinary sequence of human activity,
already extending back to about the end of the Ice Age, has been found.'

The Advertiser, Adelaide, 18 January 1960.

and their attitudes to the importance of Aborigines in Australian history?

2 There are a number of books of Aboriginal legends. Refer especially to the books by Jennifer Isaacs, *Australian Dreaming: 40 000 years of Aboriginal History*, and Ainslie Roberts and C.P. Mountford, *The Dreamtime, The Dawn of Time*, and *The First Sunrise*, which contain Aboriginal myths and illustrations referring to the creation period.

What are some of the main features and happenings of that period as revealed in these books?

3 Read the newspaper report on the opposite page about archaeological research.

What do archaeologists try to do?

What do they look for?

What are some of the questions that archaeologists are trying to answer about early Aboriginal life in Australia?

What important discoveries have they been able to make so far about the history of Aborigines in Australia?

Make a diagram or model in clay of an archaeological digging to illustrate how an archaeologist works.

4 Write a research report about the Lake Mungo discoveries, giving details of what has been found there. (See Josephine Flood *Archaeology of the Dreamtime* (rev. edn), Angus and Robertson, Sydney, 1995.)

Why are the finds at Lake Mungo so important?

5 Explain each of the following terms
   a radiocarbon dating
   b ice age
   c firestick farming
   d megafauna

6 What various explanations have been given about how Aborigines could have first arrived in Tasmania? Explain what differences there were between the traditional societies of Tasmania and the Australian mainland.

7 Can you suggest why Aborigines were the sole residents in Australia for so long?

What can you find out about the Macassan seamen who visited Australia? (Find Macassar on the island of Sulawezi on a map.)

8 In this chapter there has been discussion about what evidence can be found in relation to the Aborigines of earlier times. What evidence survives in your own district of traditional Aboriginal society?

What was the name of the local Aboriginal group? What evidence of campsites can you find? Are there any local names of Aboriginal origin, and what are the meanings of these names?

Have any forms of Aboriginal art or material culture of traditional society survived in your own district?

Chapter 2

1 What were some of the main ways in which the Aborigines adapted to living in the Australian environment?

2 Make a list of methods by which water could be obtained by the Aborigines.

3 Find out what kinds of food were available to Aborigines living in traditional manner in your locality. If this cannot be found out exactly, it should be possible to work out the likely food available, basing ideas on the type of country, nearness to rivers or the sea, climate, and other factors. (Books in the Reading List will help, and see the list given by the explorer E.J. Eyre below.)

Amongst the almost unlimited catalogue of edible articles used by the natives of Australia, the following may be classed as the chief:- all salt and fresh-water fish and shell-fish, of which, in the larger rivers, there are vast numbers and many species; fresh-water turtle; frogs of different kinds; rats and mice; lizards, and most kinds of snakes and reptiles; grubs of all kinds; moths of several varieties; fungi, and many sorts of roots; the leaves and tops of a variety of plants; the leaf and fruit of the mesembryanthemum; various kinds of fruits and berries; the bark from the roots of many trees and shrubs; the seeds of leguminous plants; gum from several species of acacia; different sorts of manna; honey from the native bee and also from the flowers of the Banksia, by soaking them in water; the tender leaves of the grass-tree; the larvae of insects; white ants; eggs of birds; turtles or lizards; many kinds of kangaroo; opossums; squirrels, sloths, and

wallabies; ducks; geese; teal; cockatoos; parrots; wild dogs and wombats; the native companion; the wild turkey; the swan; the pelican; the leipoa, and an endless variety of water-fowl, and other descriptions of birds.
E.J. Eyre: *Journals of Expeditions of Discovery into Central Australia* . . . London, 1845, Vol. 2, pp. 250–51.

Discuss the ability of the Aborigines to find food.
The following statement, representing the Aboriginal view, should be noted:

Our laws of the dreamtime tell us to hunt all creatures and food by studying their habits and lives. The flowers tell us when to hunt, the traditions of the tribe tell us where we must go to find our food.
. . . This is our land; it is our flesh and our life, and gives its secrets to those it knows and understands.
W.E. Harney: *Brimming Billabongs*, Rigby, Adelaide, 1969, p. 50.

4 Make a model of a traditional Aboriginal campsite, using only materials that would have been available to the people (or make a drawing or plan). To do this accurately, find out first what materials would have been used for shelters or huts, where fires would be located in the camp, how many people would have been in it, where weapons would have been evident, etc. (Photographs in this book will help.)

5 The illustration on page 147 shows the following material objects:
a quartzite knife in a sheath of paper bark, and the same knife withdrawn from the sheath
a hardwood *coolamon* or *pitchi*
a spindle, with string made from human hair
small musical clapping sticks
a net bag made from bark fibre, animal fur, or reeds.

What would each of these objects have been used for?
How would the knife and the *coolamon* have been made?
Which material seems to have been of greatest use to Aborigines in traditional society, and why?

6 Read the statement on pages 147–48 about Aboriginal trading practices in the Northern Territory, to help answer the question below:

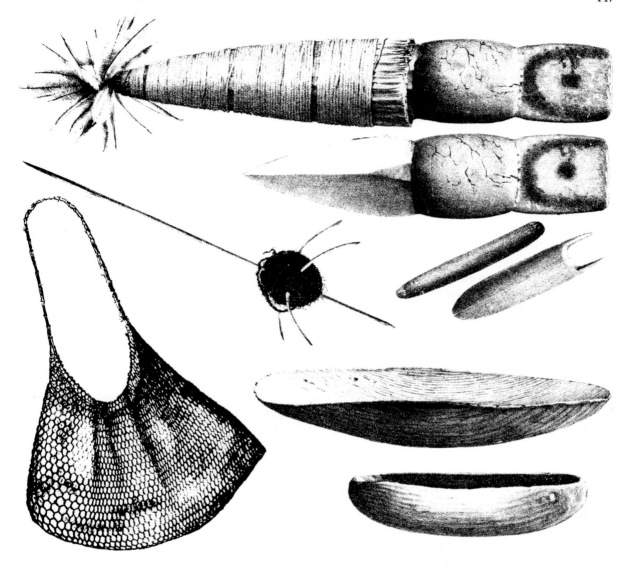

At the big coroborees of the tribes, we would trade with the natives of distant lands, who brought songs as well as goods to exchange. The trade routes were laid down in the dreamtime, and over them come the trading natives at a season when food is plentiful. When the flying-foxes come down the streams from the gorges in the hills and pass the big lily pools in our tribal land, the old men heed the sign, and the tribe moves out to the places where tradition demands that the young men shall be initiated into the secrets of tribal lore.

The tribes would muster at Nuringman, where the trade routes meet at a spot on the Victoria River, for here they

had met since the dawn of time. From sunrise way would
come the people of Wonga songs, with their special trade
of bamboo spears and long throwing sticks. From sundown
way would come the natives of the Buradjun songs, with
delicately shaped spears fashioned like leaves, and pearl
shell pendants called 'jakole' that are said to be the ears of
dead Rainbows who dwell in the lands of the big salt
waters. From the south would come the tribes of the
Iraperinji songs, with stone axes and flaked stone knives
with spinifex wax handles. Charrada singing native traders
would bring love charms of white clay called 'jerri jerri',
and red ochre, and possum aprons for women and men;
and the Wallacka natives of the Katherine River side would
bring in boomerangs and shields. So also came the natives
of Leira, Weba, Jungaree, and Bungal. Each song had its
own trade, and the relationship between song and
commodity was so fixed in the tribes that the song name
really meant the trade goods.
W.E. Harney: *Brimming Billabongs*, Rigby, Adelaide, 1969,
p. 64.

What can you find out about Aboriginal trade, the
goods and practices traded, and the extent of trade
and its importance?
7 How effective were Aborigines in satisfying their
material needs?

Chapter 3

1 What were the main characteristics of the period of
childhood in traditional Aboriginal life?
2 Find out what you can about each of the following
groups: the language ('tribal') group, the clan, the
local group, the elders.
3 Describe the role and importance of women in
traditional Aboriginal society.
4 Read the following passage:

No English words are good enough to give a sense of the
links between an Aboriginal group and its homeland. Our
word 'home', warm and suggestive though it be, does not
match the aboriginal word that may mean 'camp', 'hearth',
'country', 'everlasting home', 'totem place', 'life source',
'spirit centre' and much else all in one. Our word 'land' is
too spare and meagre. We can now scarcely use it except
with economic overtones unless we happen to be poets.

The Aboriginal would speak of 'earth' and use the word in a richly symbolic way to mean his 'shoulder' or his 'side'. I have seen an Aboriginal embrace the earth he walked on. To put our words 'home' and 'land' together into 'homeland' is a little better but not much. A different tradition leaves us tongueless and earless towards this other world of meaning and significance. When we took what we call 'land' we took what to them meant hearth, home, the source and locus of life, and everlastingness of spirit.

W.E.H. Stanner: *After the Dreaming*, Australian Broadcasting Commission, Sydney, 1969, p. 44.

From what can be understood about the relationship between Aborigines and the land, why might an Aborigine embrace the earth, as recorded above?

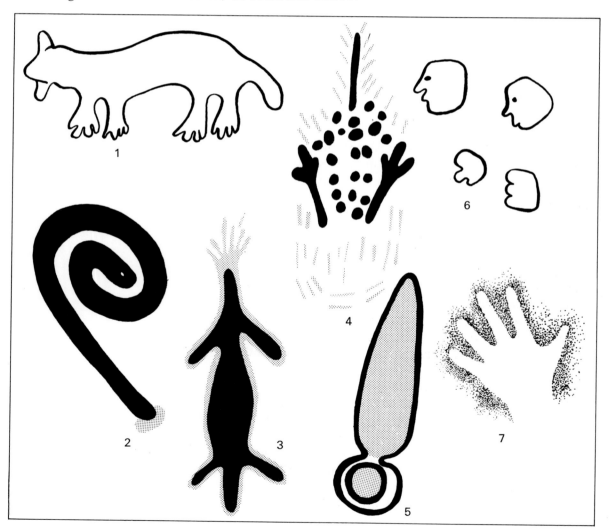

5 Explain what Aborigines in their traditional life have
  believed about
  a what happens at death
  b sicknesses and Aboriginal doctors
6 What is the purpose of ritual in traditional
  Aboriginal societies?
7 The illustration on page 149 represents a collection
  of Aboriginal rock paintings. Can you identify the
  objects painted? (Use your imagination with No. 4!
  Answers are given at the end of these Research
  Exercises.)
8 Explain the methods used in painting and
  engraving. What is the purpose of such art?

Chapter 4

1 Can you suggest why European navigators who
  visited Australia before 1788 held varying views
  about Aboriginal people and their society?
2 Make a list of the reasons for the breaking down of
  traditional Aboriginal societies in the 1788–1840
  period. Which reasons do you consider the most
  important?
3 What intentions towards the Aborigines are revealed
  in the following statements? Can you suggest why
  such intentions were not carried out in practice?

Part of the Letters Patent issued by the British
government in 1836 to establish the province of
South Australia:

NOW KNOW YE that . . . We do hereby erect and
establish one Province to be called the Province of SOUTH
AUSTRALIA—And we do hereby fix the Boundaries of the
said Province . . .
PROVIDED ALWAYS that nothing in these our Letters
Patent contained shall affect or be construed to affect the
rights of any Aboriginal Natives of the said Province to the
actual occupation or enjoyment in their own persons or in
the persons of their descendants of any lands therein now
actually occupied or enjoyed by such Natives . . .

Part of Governor Hindmarsh's First Proclamation to
South Australian colonists, 28 December 1836:

It is also, at this time especially, my duty to apprise the
Colonists of my resolution to take every lawful means for

extending the same protection to the NATIVE
POPULATION as to the rest of His Majesty's Subjects, and
of my firm determination to punish with exemplary severity
all acts of violence or injustice which may in any manner
be practised or attempted against the NATIVES, who are to
be considered as much under the Safeguard of the law as
the Colonists themselves, and equally entitled to the
privileges of British Subjects.

4 What can you find out about contacts between
Aborigines and early white settlers in your own
district?
5 The white artist who drew the picture below in the
mid-nineteenth century entitled it simply *Civilisation
vs Nature*. What other titles could have been given to
it, and why?
6 What was the policy of 'soothing the dying pillow'?
Why did some whites come to believe in it?
7 What were the general aims of the protection
policies adopted after 1900? Why did many
Aborigines resent these policies?
8 Discuss the statement of the Aborigines' Progressive
Association at the end of Chapter 4.

Chapter 5

1 Explain the terms 'restrictive laws' and 'assimilation' in regard to Aborigines. What have been some of the criticisms made about each of these practices?
2 Examine the land rights disputes before 1990 outlined in this chapter. Can you explain why state and federal governments acted so slowly in these disputes? If you were a lawyer presenting a case in favour of Aboriginal land rights, what points would you put forward?
3 What did the Mabo judgment say? Why is it so important?
4 Why has Aboriginal ill health become such a difficult issue since the white occupation of Australia began?
5 What is meant by the term 'reconciliation'? What do you think can be done to promote reconciliation between Aborigines and non-Aborigines?
6 Compile a scrapbook of newspaper cuttings relating to Aboriginal affairs. What are the main issues being described?

Identification of rock paintings, Chapter 3 Exercise 7

1 A dingo (originally drawn in charcoal outline).
2 A snake (shown emerging from a hole).
3 A lizard.
4 An emu sitting on its eggs, as seen from below (a Central Australian painting).
5 A stone knife and handle.
6 Human heads (originally outlined in charcoal).
7 A human hand (an outline formed by blowing charcoal or ochre over the hand).

Index